This edition published 1975 by
Mills and Boon Limited,
17–19 Foley Street, London W1A 1DR

ISBN 0 263 06010 1

© Sackett Publishing Services Ltd. 1975

Filmset by Ramsay Typesetters
(Crawley) Ltd, through Reynolds Clark
Associates Ltd, London
Printed in Italy by New Interlitho S.P.A.

Sure and Simple Series
created and produced by
Sackett Publishing Services Ltd,
104 Great Portland Street, London W1N 5PE

SURE & SIMPLE
HOMEMAKING

Jill Blake

Illustrated by Terry Burton

Designed by
Keith Groom and Cyril Mason

Mills & Boon Limited

London

CONTENTS

SURE & SIMPLE HOMEMAKING

Making Your House Into a Home

Homemaking is an art which comes naturally to some people — they instinctively know how to plan a room, which colours to put together, which textures to include in a scheme, where to use pattern and where to use plain surfaces, how to arrange furniture and how to add those extra finishing touches which give a home that extra special 'something'. Other people do not find the subject so easy, but all these skills can be acquired and that is what this book is all about — to help you to be your own interior designer. Over the years I have answered many letters on homemaking and interior decoration, as well as lecturing to various women's organizations on the subject and giving personal advice to people with decorating problems. I have written this book to help answer some of the many questions I have been asked.

You will find it will help you to plan your home to suit your family's particular needs and requirements; to choose colour schemes and match colours; to mix pattern and plain and textures; to plan new decor round existing items; to cope with problem rooms; to select carpets and floorcoverings; to light your rooms; to extend your home and make it more spacious; to 'dress' your windows and make curtains and blinds; to do simple upholstery; to make loose and bedcovers; to add individual 'accents' and accessories . . . but above all I hope it will help you to obtain maximum enjoyment from homemaking, for planning and decorating a home should

be fun — and so should living in it!

If you lack confidence, tackle the problem room-by-room with the help of this book. With a little practice you will be able to develop your own tastes, impress your personality on your surroundings and make your house into a home.

The two kitchen/dining rooms illustrated look absolutely super, yet they are totally different in style. In each case structural changes were made, a wall was removed to create more space, and both schemes have been planned as practical, dual-purpose rooms. Yet one is streamlined and modern, suitable for a busy family-in-a-hurry;

and the other is traditional, the real heart-of-the-home, an inviting room in which to enjoy cooking and eating country fare. The two completely contrasting schemes show how rooms can have completely different atmospheres, depending on the likes, dislikes and personality of the owner. Neither room just 'happened', they are both the result of careful planning. Textures, colours, pattern and plain surfaces, pieces of furniture . . . all have been skilfully blended and the accessories in both schemes chosen to provide the perfect finishing touches — both are superb examples of the art of homemaking.

Where Do I Start?

When it comes to planning and decorating a few lucky people have a natural flair and can transform a room with a speed and ease that is staggering. Most of us are not so fortunate, and I hope this book will help you to avoid costly mistakes. As the most important thing is to plan your home for happy living, you will have to sit down and make a master plan room-by-room.

First of all you should think about the needs of all the people who are going to live in your home, whether it be a flat, bungalow, suburban 'semi' or rambling country vicarage! Obviously a couple with young children have to compromise when planning schemes for areas which are common to all members of the family (hall, stairs, kitchen, bathroom, living room) — consequently these are the places to use washable wall surfaces, hardwearing and easy-to-clean floorings and fabrics, robust furniture and practical colours. This does not mean every room has to be child-proof! The main bedroom, for example, can be decorated in formal style with fragile fabrics and shaggy carpets in pastel colours.

It is possible to re-think the purpose of some rooms — in a house with two reception rooms, it may be practical to make one a family living room and the other an 'adults only' drawing room. Or you may decide to use the second downstairs room as a playroom with bunk beds and turn the largest bedroom into an upstairs sitting room (think of Regency houses with first floor drawing rooms). If you have one open-plan room downstairs then this could be a family living room with the main bedroom doubling as an adult sitting room or study (for more ideas see Chapter 8). The important thing is to maintain a flexible approach to your home and not to be too tied by convention.

Having decided on the purpose and function of the various rooms and whether the decorations are to be practical or more sophisticated, you now need to get down to the really practical side of planning. First arm yourself with the right tools for the job! You will need: A large exercise book (preferably with squared paper), or sheets of squared graph paper; a ruler with imperial and metric measurements; a setsquare; pencils (black and coloured); steel measuring tape (cloth ones stretch with use); pieces of stiff card, clips, pins and sticky tape for making colour boards (see Chapter 2); paint manufacturer's paint 'chips'; colour samples of any existing items to be incorporated; a folder in which to keep brochures or colour photographs cut from magazines. This equipment will enable you to plan your home room-by-room and serve as a permanent record to help you with re-decorating later.

The tools of the trade — these are needed for making a master plan of each room in your house. Even if you are tackling one room at a time, you still need to make an overall plan so the finished results all blend together to create an harmonious whole.

You will need to measure each room very carefully, then draw it out to scale on the squared paper; half an inch to one foot (1:25 cm) is the usual scale, although you can adjust this to suit yourself.

Mark all the measurements on the plan including length, breadth, height, the positions and sizes of doors and windows (with sill height from the floor), and all other relevant information.

How Do I Make a Master Plan?

You may be starting completely from scratch with a new home and furniture, or moving house and have to fit in most of your existing pieces, or you may simply be redecorating one room — whichever is your particular problem you still need to start with the steel measuring tape, the squared paper, setsquare, ruler and pencil (see previous page). **1** Measure your room very carefully, then draw it out to scale on your squared paper, making one square (or half an inch) equal to one foot. Indicate recesses, doors, windows — and which way they open, as well as positioning any fitted furniture. **2** Next measure up any existing items of furniture, draw them out to the same scale, colour and cut out. **3** Move the cut-outs round on your room plan until you get a practical and happy arrangement, then stick them down in position.

There are certain basic measurements which have to be considered: In the sitting room for example, make sure there is enough room to walk round chairs and tables, and that the television set can be seen by everybody without major upheaval; in the dining room

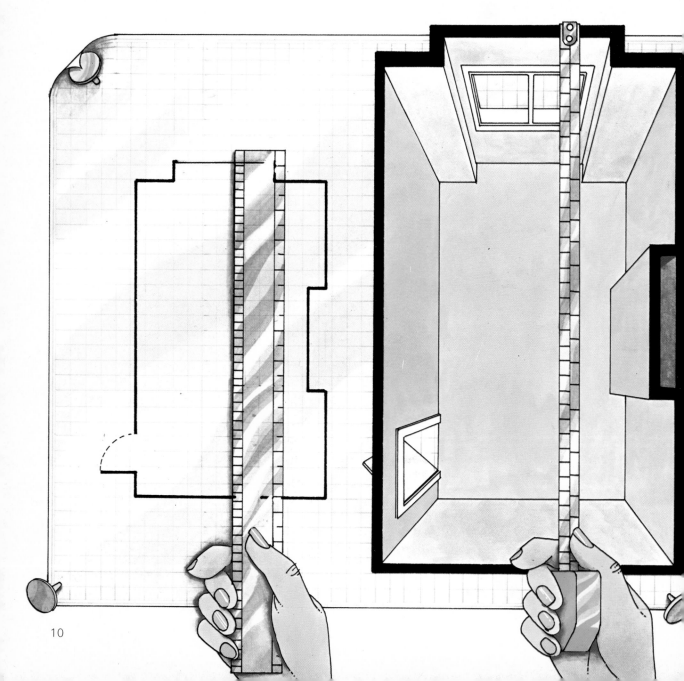

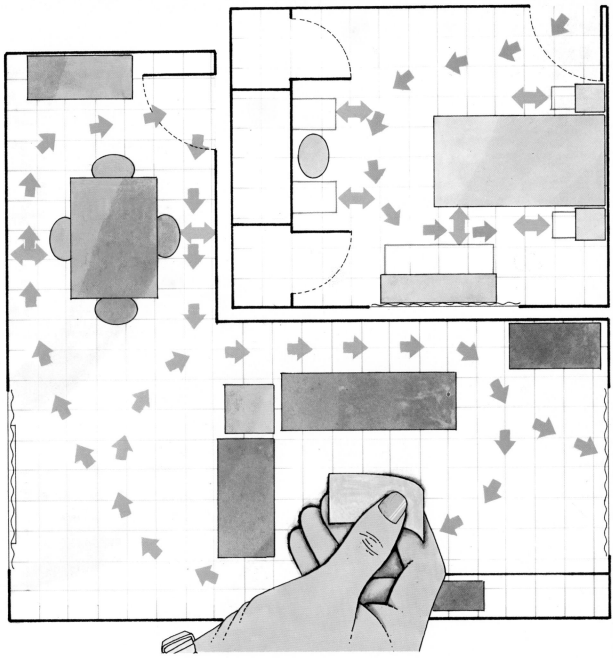

there must be adequate room to get round the table and chairs for easy serving — chairs also should not touch the wall when their occupants push them back to get up from the table. In the bedroom, check that you can walk past the bottom of the bed easily, be able to pull it out for bed-making, *and* be able to open doors of wardrobes and drawers of chests without knocking them against other furniture.

Incidentally, if you are buying new furniture you can still do this — measure up the items in the shop, or check the sizes in the manufacturer's catalogue, then draw and cut out the shapes to scale as before.

Now is the time to think about the lighting — you will need lamps, wall lights, ceiling fittings and possibly some concealed lighting. All this will have to be considered in relation to the furniture. When you have stuck your furniture cut-outs in position on your master room plan, you will then know exactly where you need your lights and can make any necessary alterations to switches and sockets *before* you start the redecoration. *Note.* This method of planning is ideal when you move house, since it enables you to know exactly where each piece is to go and the removal men will be able to position the furniture easily. You will also be able to discard any pieces which are too large for the new home before you move!

Structural Alterations

room floor or having to remove sweet wrappings from a chair before you can sit down! It may be more practical to make an opening large enough to take double, folding or sliding doors, so the entire area can be opened up when necessary, but at other times some members of the

family can have privacy behind the doors while others are watching television or listening to music.

If your room is already open-plan and you have discovered the disadvantages, then you may be able to divide it by the methods above, or less permanently with fold-back louvred doors, vertical venetian blinds, or full-length curtains, mounted on ceiling track. If the room is not large enough to divide, then you can at least 'zone' the areas by the clever positioning of your furniture (see page 28), or you may be able to add on an extension (see Chapter 8), and then divide the whole area. In some older houses there is often a kitchen or breakfast room and small scullery, side-by-side. Here it may well make sense to create one open-plan kitchen and a breakfast or family-meals area. A word of warning — if you study

Structural alterations' can cover a number of quite different building jobs, from replacing a window or removing a fireplace to knocking down walls to make open-plan areas. Installing central heating also comes under the heading of 'structural changes'. You will find a master plan, drawn to scale, helps you get down to the practical aspects of planning such alterations and can save time and money in the long run! But before you seriously consider undertaking major structural work, such as removing internal walls, first ask yourself whether one large living area will suit you and your family. Big 'through' rooms can be elegant and spacious if the family consists mainly of adults, or you are all fantastically tidy, but there is nothing worse than falling over children's toys littering the living

the pros and cons and then decide you still want to take a sledge hammer to one of your internal walls, it may be load-bearing so you will have to seek the advice of a competent builder, surveyor or architect, who will also advise about strengthening the opening with an RSJ, and also about local Building Regulations, and whether it is necessary to obtain planning permission.

The magnificent open-plan living area (far left) shows how effective structural alterations can be — the door from the hall has been removed and replaced by an arched entrance — the shape is echoed in the curved frame of the mirror. The sitting area is slightly sunken, thereby 'zoning' the areas without spoiling the visual appearance of space and light, which is further emphasized by the subtle colour scheme and clever mixture of patterned and plain surfaces.

If you feel large 'through' rooms are not practical, then you can compromise with folding or sliding doors between the two areas (bottom far left), but the two schemes should blend together.

In an older-style house there may be a small breakfast room and scullery — here (see above) they have been made into one kitchen and dining area, but part of the wall was retained and now makes a practical place for a family message board.

In a terrace house with a very narrow hall it may be possible to remove part of the wall between the hall and one of the downstairs rooms, but this area could be cold in winter — adding a porch onto the front door would help keep out draughts. The way the walls have been painted (bottom left) with very definite horizontal bands of colour, and the striped effect created by laying two tones of carpet tiles all help to create a feeling of space and greater width.

How do I Shop for Colour?

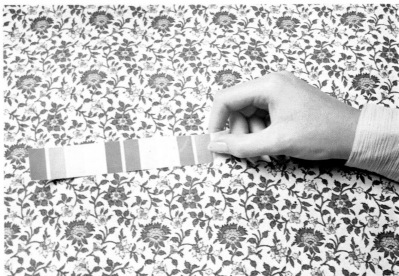

Colour-planning is also an integral part of successful home planning — in fact it is such an important part Chapter 2 is entirely devoted to choosing colour schemes and on the next page you will see how to make a colour board to take with you when you shop. You will notice reference is made to paint manufacturer's colour chips, and they certainly can be a great help with colour-matching. These helpful charts are becoming more sophisticated all the time: some manufacturers group the different tones of each colour together on one page, one provides a card with little windows through which you can see toning or 'companion' colours, another makes a 'dial-a-colour selector' with revolving discs, enabling you to choose contrasting or toning schemes, but probably the most helpful is the type of paint card where you can tear off a strip of similarly matched colours and use them for colour-matching when you shop, and as an integral part of your colour board. You see them illustrated in action here, at the same time proving how easy it is to work several schemes round one existing item, such as tan-brown upholstery!

Top left. There are many tones

the upholstery and the rug.

The final effect is bright, warm and cheerful — the woodwork has been painted to match the walls, making the room seem larger, and a colour contrast has been introduced in the curtains which are turquoise and gold on white — they make the golden walls glow even more! *Below*. Richly patterned curtain fabric can be difficult to work into a scheme — sometimes the answer is to select one colour from the fabric for carpet, another for walls and a third for upholstery.

In this room the subtle coffee-beige walls tone with the curtain

and shades of green, and colour-matching can be quite difficult, especially as some greens look quite different in daylight from artificial light. If you decide on a restful scheme, and want 'Chartreuse' green walls, you can use the strips of colour to select a

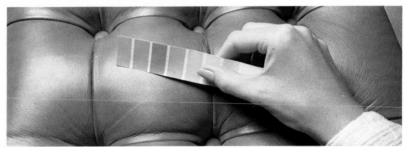

fabric without actually matching it, and echo the soft beige floor covering. Again the rich golden-tan upholstery blends well with the scheme. Touches of red in the accessories add depth to the scheme, and contrast with the beige and tan tones.

curtain fabric to echo the wall colour. Alternatively, if you are starting with a patterned curtain fabric you can hold the paint chips up against it to help you choose a wall colour. In the finished room scheme, the green is contrasted with lots of white, the tan-brown leather upholstery gives warmth to the schemes and the rug echoes both the green and the tan, and helps to make the room appear wider. *Above*. Starting with the same tan-brown leather for upholstery, you may prefer a sunny scheme — the colour chips help you to select a wall colour such as 'Corn' yellow, to blend with

Help Please – I'm Hopeless with Colour!

When colour is skillfully used it can improve the atmosphere and proportions of almost any room, yet colour itself costs absolutely nothing! An expensively furnished drawing room may look drab and dreary, whilst a bedsitter decorated on a shoestring can be fabulous if the colour scheme is right.

There are many different ways of actually working out a colour scheme, but, as I emphasized in the preceding chapter, planning is all-important if the finished results are not to be a hit-and-miss affair. If you have begun at the beginning, then you will have decided on any structural changes, drawn out a scale plan of your room and stuck down drawings of the furniture in their proposed positions. Armed with this and your colour board (see right) you are ready to go 'shopping for samples'.

If you have to plan the new scheme round an existing item (see Chapter 4) pin a colour-guide to this on the board. Obviously you cannot cut a lump off a fitted carpet or hack a piece out of the suite, so when necessary colour-match to pieces of wool, embroidery silks or paint manufacturer's colour chips (pick up a colour chart at your local D.I.Y. or decorating shop). If the item you want to include in the new scheme is patterned, half-close your eyes to judge the pre-dominant colour and take a much larger sample of that tone. Build up the board with cuttings of items you see and like in the shops.

Sometimes it is not pos-sible to get a sample there and then, but if you want to avoid costly mistakes, ask the assistant to obtain a sample for you, or get the name and address of the manufacturer and write to him direct with full details of the style name (or number) and colourway.

Once the board is complete, take it home and look at it in the room in which you intend to use the scheme. As most colours look quite different in artificial light, daylight and so-called 'daylight' lighting in shops, you may find some of the samples don't match properly in your own domestic lighting — some tones of green for example can look grey in artificial light. Also look at floorcovering samples at right angles to the window and hold curtain fabric up against the light.

When you are perfectly happy with your sampled colour scheme you can then go ahead and order the materials, get down to decorating and finally enjoy living in your new sur-roundings.

It is absolutely impossible to carry colour in your eye, so work out your colour scheme the way the professional decor-ators do, by making a colour board. It is not at all difficult — all you need is a piece of stiff card, a stout metal clip, a pencil for notes, a few pins or clips and some sticky tape. Pin on your scale plan, samples of any exist-ing items (or colour guide to them) and as you shop around add cuttings of wallcoverings, carpet, fabrics, paint, etc.

If you lack confidence, want the opinions of the whole family, or simply enjoy playing with colour, you can make two or three colour boards for one room. When they are finished, leave them in the room for a few days until you reach a decision on which is the most effective.

Note. When colour-matching don't rely on printed leaflets — however well-produced they are the colour is not always true and you could find you had based your scheme on entirely the wrong colour — this is equally true of brochures showing bathroom fittings, tiles and kitchen units, as of catalogues of furniture, carpets, and fabrics, so ask your shop to get you a proper sample.

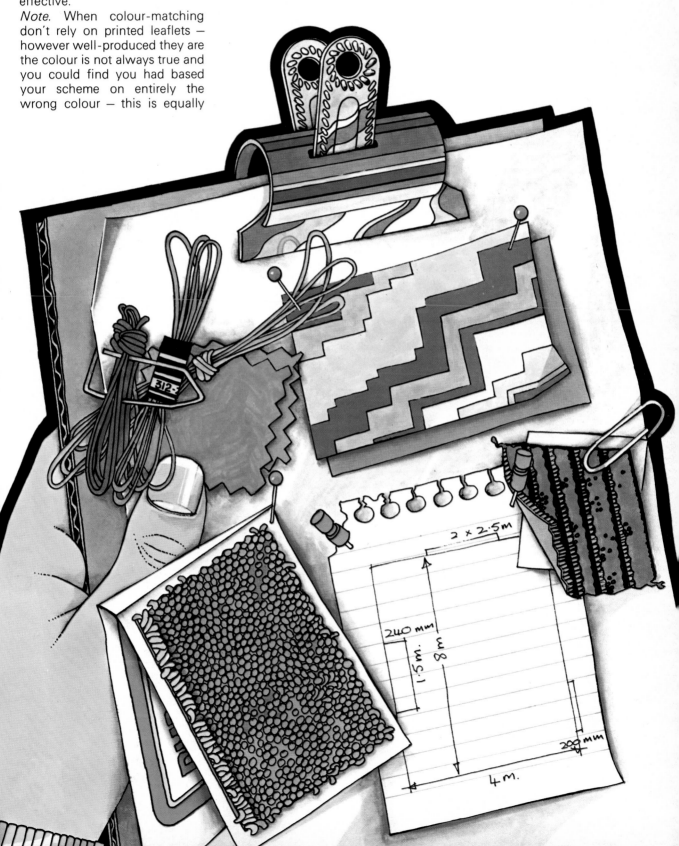

How do I Choose a Colour Scheme?

Colour scheming should be fun, but many people are afraid of making a mistake and so 'play safe' with dull or neutral colours! It is possible to save a dull scheme (see page 30), but why not start off with a really attractive blend of colours?

First, look at the colour wheels below; one wheel shows the primary colours of red, yellow and blue and the other shows the secondary colours (or colours of the rainbow as they are often called). These are made from mixing the primary colours together so we have red and yellow making orange, yellow and blue making green and red and blue making violet. From these basic colours spring all the various shades, tints and tones of colour from vivid scarlet to palest lemon, from rich aubergine-purple to fragile leaf green.

The colours on the second wheel to the *right* of the dotted line are the warm colours and to the *left* are the cold colours. As some greeny-yellows and golds can be cold, and some violets can be warm the dotted line sub-divides these two sections. You may wonder what difference it makes whether colours are warm or cold, but it is most important to choose the warm colours for cold cheerless rooms (those which face north, east or north-east) and to select cooler colours for the warmer south, west or south-west facing rooms.

To create a really successful scheme, introduce some clear, sharp, cold colours into a warm scheme and some rich, hot shades into a room decorated in cool colours. These contrasting 'accent' colours help to emphasise the warm or cool effect of the scheme and can be introduced in accessories such as cushions, lampshades, pictures, glass, books and ornaments, or as an integral part of the scheme in a chair, rug, contrasting wall or curtains.

Colours also have different tones, which means they can be light or dark. The pale colours retreat, so they make walls appear further away and ceilings look higher, consequently these are ideal for use in small, dark, box-like rooms — they also reflect light and so make the most of daylight and artificial light, creating a really bright atmosphere, particularly in old, dark houses. Dark colours work in the opposite way, they advance, making walls and ceilings seem nearer to you than they actually are; consequently they can be used to make large areas appear cheerful and welcoming — they are particularly effective used in very big entrance halls or on tall ceilings to make them appear lower. Again a combination of both types of colour in a room creates a much more interesting scheme.

There are also 'neutral' colours — tones such as grey and beige are often called neutral colours, but in fact only black and white are true neutrals. Grey and beige tones are the hardest colours to match as they can be blue-grey, blue-beige, green-grey and green-beige on the cold side, and pink-grey, yellow-grey, pink-beige and yellow-beige on the warm side. It is possible to work out some very elegant tone-on-tone schemes with these colours (see page 24).

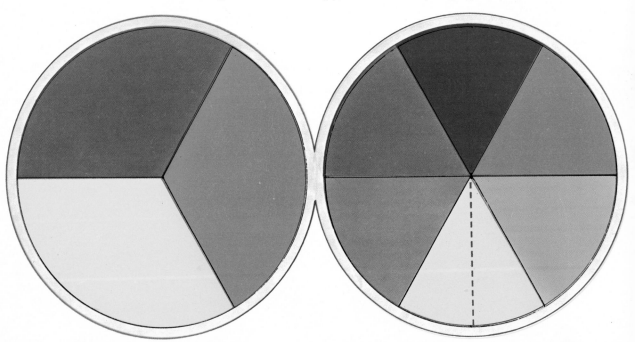

The elegant blue and green drawing room (below) is a typical example of cool colours, skilfully used to create a feeling of light and spaciousness. The white coving and paintwork give added crispness to the scheme, and a warm colour note is introduced in pink flowers and accessories. The modern living room (bottom left) is a complete contrast — rich, warm colours have been used as a perfect foil to the stark modern furniture — the golden tan and red in the wallcovering have been picked up in carpet, blind and bookcase, with white and grey used as cool accents. The third room (bottom right) is mainly in tones of cool greens and olives with a bronze-gold carpet. The effect could have been chilly, but warmth is introduced in the upholstered couch in burnt-orange velvet, and golden-yellow accessories. Cushions could be added in tones of green, olive, gold and apricot, with possibly a little sharp peacock blue.

Where do I use Cool Colours?

First of all, we need to establish exactly which are the cool colours! Blue of course, and blue-greens; nearly all the greens until they turn to a golden-green shade; bluish-purple; violet and lilac until they begin to show a hint of pink; most greys (unless they have a lot of pink or yellow mixed with them); some beige tones; black and white — although strictly speaking these last two are 'non' colours.

All these colours are suitable for use in warm rooms, and here the aspect of your house has to be taken into consideration. Your neighbour across the road may well have used blues and greens most successfully in her sitting room, which faces west, but if you try to repeat the effect in your room, which faces east you could be very disappointed. The cool colours look best in the rooms which are warm and sunny — which face south, west or south-west and get the sunshine from midday onwards.

The pale, cool tones are ideal for rooms with large windows overlooking the garden, conservatories and extensions, where you are aiming to create a feeling of space and light and want to link the room visually with the garden or intend to use a lot of house plants. Cool colours can also look marvellous in small, pokey bedrooms, particularly sparse attics or chalet-bungalow rooms with sloping ceilings, which can get oppressively hot in summer (see page 58). The vivid cool colours such as lime green used with purples, peacocks and turquoise, are very effective in children's rooms, kitchens and bathrooms where you want a really fresh, clean crisp atmosphere.

The 'garden' room (above left) in a large, old house is also used as a dining room. The colour scheme, entirely based on green, white and soft beige is almost stark in its simplicity — painted walls, vinyl flooring,

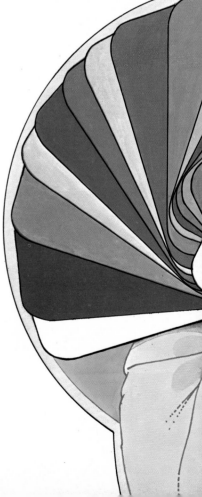

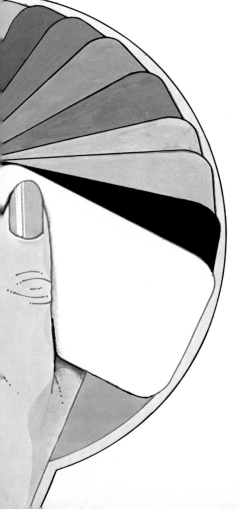

rattan blinds and masses of plants. A few touches of tangerine-orange help emphasise the cool effect. But, if you turn the page you will see the same room, decorated in warm colours and looking quite different!

The more conventional sitting room (above) in shades of soft-green and turquoise with lots of white shows how pale, cool colours and muted designs can make a small and rather ordinary room appear spacious, and an ideal place in which to relax.

The bedroom (top right), in shades of lilac, blue and white looks cool and inviting — the softly draped window and bed-cover give added softness to the scheme.

Most halls need to be warm and welcoming, but this one (bottom right), faces south-west and needed a cool touch so the walls were decorated with a vinyl wallcovering in shades of olive, lilac and blue — the lilac echoed in a roller blind, the olive in the floor tiles.

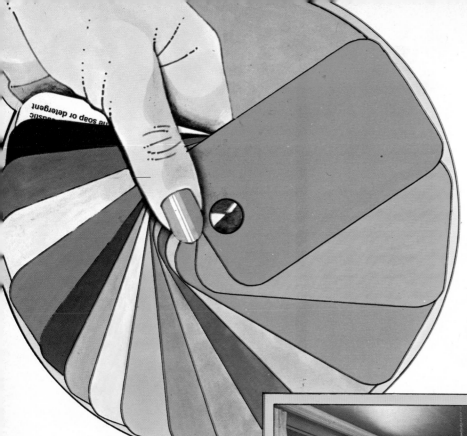

exactly how important colour is in creating atmosphere. Even though the flooring is in tones of black, white and grey, the ceiling painted grey and the walls banded with grey, the overall effect is of warmth because red is such a strong colour.

The bedroom scheme (top right), is based on cream and cognac brown, but sharp emerald green has been introduced in curtains and accessories to add a colour contrast and to emphasise the rich, warm effect of the other tones.

Some greens can be warm-looking if they are in the golden-olive colour group. In this sitting room (far right), the wallpaper is in shades of pink and red, but also has touches of the green-

What Colours do I use in a Cold Room?

Chilly, damp or dark rooms need bright, warm cheerful colour schemes and so this means choosing colours from the warm side of the colour wheel. Red is probably the warmest colour of all, closely followed by orange; apricots; golds; most of the yellow tones (except for those which are greenish); purplish-reds; lilac-pinks; pink; rich browns; tans; cream; all the range of autumnal colours. Many natural surfaces have a pleasing warmth of their own — wood used on walls as cladding and for flooring, as well as in furniture; cork in all its tones from rich brownish-black to honey-gold; most natural brick surfaces; the soft, creamy

colours of wool (found in carpets and upholstery fabrics), sisal and rush, rattan or cane — all these can be used to help give warmth to a cold room (see more about natural textures on page 40).

This rich, warm, inviting dining room is in fact exactly the same room as the cool green one on the previous page and proves

olive in it, linking with the upholstery colour. The reds and pinks are echoed in accessories such as cushions, flowers and ornaments.

Natural wood has a warmth all of its own as can be seen in this country-style kitchen (below right). The red and white painted walls and accessories emphasize the rich, cosy effect.

Tone-on-Tone Colour Schemes

Some very effective rooms are based on different tones of one colour. The finished result is usually very restful, but the atmosphere can be warm or cold, depending on the colours chosen. If you decide on this type of scheme the colours need to be very skilfully blended and there should be a contrast between the light and dark tones of the colour. For example if you decide to decorate a room in blues, and to use tones of navy, Royal and Wedgwood, a little sharp turquoise will give the scheme extra life — or if you choose shades of coffee and chocolate use beige and creamy-white as a contrast. Lots of sparkling white can also be used with a tone-on-tone scheme and often saves this type of room from looking rather dull.

This really beautiful farm-house kitchen has been decorated in tones of orange and the overall effect is warm and inviting. The walls and wood-work have been painted in toning colours produced specifically to go together — this manufacturer makes a colour-card for this range with little windows cut in the colour sheen paint which enable you to see the harmonising gloss colour through the cut-out. The floor-covering is a brick effect which echoes the wall and woodwork colour and introduces the sharper tangerine which is also used to paint the chairs. The natural wood tones in effectively and the few touches of white and green help 'lift' the scheme.

From the other side of the colour wheel — a bathroom (below) in shades of sky blue demonstrates a successful scheme using light and dark tones of the same colour, with just a little white. The starting point was the bath and basin in a fairly rich sky blue, the tiles are made to match, but are much lighter in tone as they are printed on a white ground. The washable cotton rug is in an even paler shade while the sloping ceiling is a really deep peacock blue. The curtains are

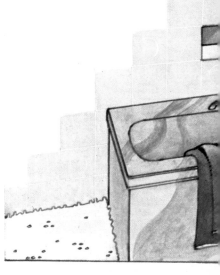

In tones of sky blue with a little lilac and accessories such as bathroom jars and towels are in tones of blue with one or two touches of lilac.

The living room (top left) in tones of beige, coffee and brown has been designed round the shaggy-piled carpet. The walls have been painted milky-coffee colour, the furniture is a warm tan-brown, curtains (not shown) echo the bitter chocolate tone — beige and creamy-white provide tonal contrast.

Grey need not be dull and drab, in fact it can be very elegant as this grey, white and silver tone-on-tone scheme proves (top right). The starting point here was the hand-blocked wallpaper, based on the design of an oak-leaf, in two tones of grey with white. The ceiling was painted pale steel-grey to tone and the curtains, with their lovely moiré texture are a shade or two darker, and edged with slightly lighter braid. All the woodwork is white and the flooring grey and white. The smoked glass table top, metal accessories and fish print all echo the grey and silver theme.

Contrasting Colour Schemes

Contrasting colour schemes are created by mixing colours from the opposite sides of the colour wheel in more-or-less equal proportions. Such schemes are ideal for rooms which are not particularly dark, cold or damp, nor very bright and sunny — in fact many rooms facing from north to south or east to west fall into this category. The important thing is to get the balance of colours right for your particular room. For a fairly light scheme, use more of a light or bright colour, while for a rich fairly warm scheme use more of the 'hot' colour. Examples are shown of contrasting colours, on which you could base a successful scheme: burnt-orange with turquoise; purple with lime green; chocolate with sky-blue; rose with olive green.

A sitting room scheme (see above) based on the contrasting colours of coral and red with tangerine and white. The wallpaper is in shades of coral, tangerine and green on white, the upholstery echoes the green in the wallpaper and the cushions link with the coral, the sheer curtains are in tangerine and the woodwork is olive — white keeps the scheme light.

The second living room setting (see below) is based on grey and red and would be ideal for a medium-sized rather dark room since the overall effect is light and bright. The wallpaper, in tones of black, white and grey links well with the silver grey upholstery — the red carpet immediately gives the room warmth and colour but is not

too dominant because of the grey and white furniture breaking up the area of solid colour. The accessories in red and white link with the rest of the scheme.

Contrasting colour schemes do not have to be very bold or dramatic — the colours can be subtle, yet very effective as the third living room picture (see left) proves. Soft pinky-lilac emulsion has been used for the walls, a toning pink for the ceiling and woodwork, and the carpet is a soft golden-green and the furniture a deeper olive green on beige. The curtains are printed in all the olive, gold and pink shades and spare fabric has been used for a lampshade.

The bathroom scheme (bottom left) is based on vivid greens, white and warm tan-browns — in a small room it is possible to use very bright contrasting colours very effectively, but they can make a room seem smaller, so the scheme must be chosen carefully, and if necessary use lots of white or mirrors strategically placed to give maximum reflected light. Here the two tones of green are used with white for the wallcovering, the towels echo the wallpaper in colour and motif, while the other surfaces are in warm tan-browns and ochre. Note the attractive towel rails made from wood curtain poles.

27

How do I Improve the Proportions of my Room?

By the clever use of colour you can make a cold room seem warmer, a small claustrophobic room appear larger and more spacious or make a dark area look lighter. With a subtle blend of pattern and plain surfaces you can play all sorts of tricks which deceive the eye: give a small box-like room character; make a forbidding high-ceilinged entrance hall appear warm and inviting; improve the proportions of a long, narrow living room. It is not always necessary to redecorate and refurnish to achieve these results — you can often improve the look of a room by moving the furniture round (use the plan method first, as described in Chapter 1), grouping it in large rooms so it breaks up the floor area and streamlining it back against the walls in small, cluttered rooms.

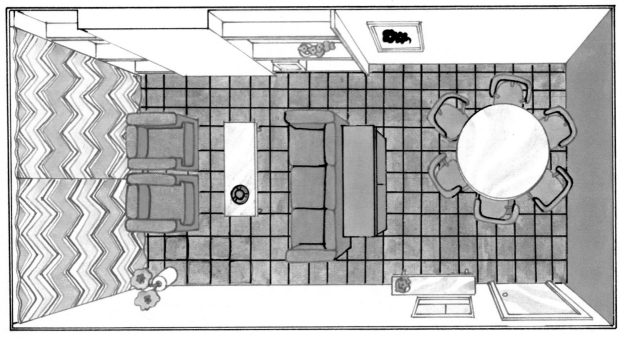

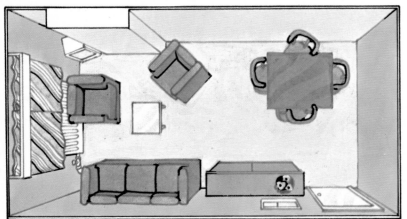

The long, narrow room, often used for both sitting and dining, can present a decoration problem. Our 'before' shows how the narrowness is emphasised by the way the furniture is arranged along the two main walls. In the 'after' picture the room takes on an entirely new personality. The settee has been placed at right-angles to the long wall with the sideboard backing it. This makes a natural, but easy-to-move division between the two areas. A new, circular table, takes up less room, yet seats six instead of four and the slim coffee table and wall units give a streamlined look. Patterned curtains cover the end wall and have a distinct horizontal design — the wall opposite the window is painted a toning, bold colour and the floorcovering treatment all help to make the room seem far less long and narrow.

Before

High-ceilinged room in an older house often seems far too tall and gives the room a cold, unfriendly atmosphere.

After

There are ways of coping with the problem! In a living room retain the picture rail, and pick it out in white, also the cornice and woodwork. The bed of the ceiling (flat part) and frieze are painted Fountain blue, the walls deep Regatta blue — the curtains have a horizontal pattern.

Before

A small, square bedroom in a modern house often lacks character.

After

Paint one wall in a bold, dramatic colour (or use patterned paper) to provide a much needed focal point and arrange a group of pictures on the bedhead wall to give added interest to the scheme.

29

What if my Finished Scheme Looks Dull?

Sometimes the most carefully planned scheme does not look quite the way you expected when the room is finished. Do not despair, it is usually possible to save the day by adding a few finishing touches which need not be at all costly! If you have a very elegant tone-on-tone scheme in shades of bronze and brown, like our sitting room (above), but the wall colour looks darker than you expected, then you can easily correct this by hanging a patterned vinyl wallcovering (or a wallpaper) which echoes the tones in the room and also introduces white. You only need to use this on one wall or in a recess or fireplace alcoves — and make it extra-easy for yourself by choosing a ready-pasted wallcovering!

In a bedroom (left) decorated in shades of pinks, beige, soft green and brown with lots of white, the whole scheme comes suddenly to life when three

cushions in green, deep rose and bronze are placed on the bed and two turquoise lampshades, on white bedside lamps, provide sharp colour contrast.

In a hall with 'Sandalwood' walls, creamy paintwork and burnt-orange carpet tiles (see right), the overall effect could be rather gloomy, but you can see how a junk shop find (an old table) and a group of pictures can create a really eye-catching effect. The table was painted 'Signal Red', prints were chosen to tone with the colour scheme and then simply framed on matching red mounts.

A subtle beige colour scheme could look very uninteresting, but the unusual introduction of purple and gold in cushions, pictures and house plants (see above), make the perfect finishing touch. Note how the purple cushions are banded with gold, and the gold cushions trimmed with matching braid. The pictures have gold-coloured mounts to tone.

Mixing Pattern and Plain

Colour is not the only thing to be taken into consideration when you are planning a successful room scheme. If all the surfaces were to be perfectly plain and similar in texture, no matter how skilfully the colours had been blended, the result would still be lifeless, dull, uninteresting . . . This does not mean you should go to the other extreme and cover everything with a riot of clashing design and texture! Like everything else, there is a happy medium.

How much pattern, or rather how many different patterns should I use in a room? This is a question which I am often asked, and until recently I would have advised using one predominant design in say wallcovering, carpet, or curtains. However, there are fashion trends in homemaking, just as there are fashion trends in clothes. Nowadays it is perfectly acceptable to wear 'co-ordinates' which often means a different pattern on each garment, yet they are specifically planned to go together and the designs are similar in feeling. Such sophisticated co-ordinates have not yet reached the furniture and allied industries, but already wallpaper, curtain and upholstery fabric, bedcovers and roller blinds are available, all designed to go together. It is largely a matter of personal taste, how many surfaces you decide to cover with the same design. Surprisingly enough if you do use wallpaper, curtains, bedcover and even loosecovers in the same pattern the effect can make a small room seem larger, so long as the design is not too overpowering.

The main problem, however, is mixing different patterns in a room when they are not really meant to go together. Here the golden rule to follow is to mix designs which are similar in feeling. You can, for example, use a neat geometric pattern on your walls, a larger geometric design on the floor and perhaps echo this in curtains. You could not blend together successfully a traditional floral carpet with a violent modern abstract curtain fabric and a Paisley-designed wallpaper — far better to have plain walls (echoing one of the colours in the carpet) and striped curtains. So, if your scheme is modern, then keep to similar modern patterns, if it is traditional try to select designs which have the same period flavour about them, and remember two florals very rarely go together unless specifically designed to do so.

Texture should also be true to type and blend with the style of the room — wood, brick, cork, chrome, glass; these harsh or natural textures go well with modern decor, while velvet, silks, satins and brass blend better with traditional schemes.

Left. The cool blue bedroom is a perfect example of two floral patterns, which are similar in feeling, blending together — yet the wallcovering and bedcover were not specifically designed to go together. The colour scheme is further enhanced by a deep purple carpet which links with the purple in the cover, and the vivid yellow accessories which provide a warm colour contrast.

Below. The sophisticated living room scheme in tones of soft coffee-beige, bitter chocolate and white shows how well stripes blend with a geometric design. The bold upholstery fabric could look very garish, but here the result is subtle and restful. The striped carpet echoes the colour of the chairs, and the chocolate wall provides a perfect plain foil to the other patterned surfaces.

Where Should I use Pattern?

If you want to use a fair amount of pattern in a room it can be difficult to decide exactly on which surface (or surfaces) to put it — visualising the finished results is another problem many people have, particularly judging

the overall effect of a fairly bold design. For example, you may choose from a small sample in a wallpaper book, only to be appalled when you see the paper hung on four walls in a small room! Bold designs, and for that matter bright colours, look two or three times as strong when seen on a large area; consequently it is best to confine the really strong patterns to an area which is fairly easy to change, unless you have a very large hall or open-plan room and want to make it look smaller. Don't buy a brightly patterned carpet unless you really feel you can live with it for many years (see 'White Elephants', page 44) instead have a two-tone or textured flooring and use the bold design on one or more walls — when you tire of it you can simply overpaint the wallpaper with emulsion, or hang a new wallcovering. Bold designs on curtains always look effective because of the 'movement' in the fabric — pattern can also be used on one chair (mix-and-match with plain loose covers), on cushions, a bedcover, roller

blind under plain curtains, even an eye-catching arrangement of a group of pictures on one wall can provide design interest for a dull room.

The soft feminine bedroom in shades of pink/mauve and white and the rich, vibrant living room in shades of pinks, gold and red show just how elegant complementary fabrics and wallpapers can look, and how effective pattern can be when used on several different surfaces in a room. Both schemes have patterned walls, curtain fabric, matching blinds and soft furnishing, but floorcoverings and other surfaces are perfectly plain. The colouring and design chosen for the bedroom is pale and delicate so the room does not appear small despite the bold use of pattern. The living room is much larger and the bold use of red for furniture and carpet with the richly designed paper and fabric create a warm, cosy atmosphere.

Pattern does not have to be confined to the living room or the bedroom — the bathroom is an ideal place in which to use strong design, since you are not looking at it all the time! Small rooms are also easy to redecorate when you tire of the decorations. The black and white bathroom scheme has been based on the tile-effect sheet vinyl flooring, and complemented with a bold 1930's Odeon-style wallpaper. The only colour is provided by green plants and red/white striped towels.

Design in the kitchen can be bold or subdued depending on the type of person you are! The orange, green and white kitchen has matching tiles — ceramic for the walls and vinyl for the floor, the result of specific cooperation on the part of two manufacturers. The dining/kitchen relies on a patterned roller blind, striped painted wall behind the work surfaces and carpet tiles laid chevron-fashion to provide design interest.

Where Should I use Plain?

If you have a very small room, then most of the surfaces should be fairly plain, although they can have an interesting texture. This makes the room appear larger, but you can introduce some really effective design into the scheme in something which is fairly easy to change. For example look at the pictures of the two bedrooms, both rooms are based on the same principle — eye-catching design for the quilt cover and bed valance,

with the remaining surfaces toning with it but not 'shouting' at it! The choice of colour and design makes one room seem bright and gay — a young person's room, and the other cool, elegant and definitely feminine.

Plain walls are a perfect foil for a collection of pictures or other *objects d'art*, and they certainly show off really beautiful antique or modern furniture to best advantage, since the eye

is not distracted by fussy detail as a background to the piece, and the pureness of line can be fully appreciated.

If you already have a patterned carpet (see page 46) or other floorcovering, it is wise to keep the rest of the scheme fairly plain, particularly if the design is rather delicate and you want to draw attention to it. This does not mean the scheme has to be dull, since you can introduce some interesting textures to bring

the scheme to life.

This unusual traditional living room (left) proves how plain walls show off pictures and good pieces of furniture to advantage. The room is particularly interesting because of the floor treatment — a sheet vinyl with a tile pattern instead of the more conventional carpet usually found in such rooms. The only pattern in the room is in this floorcovering, although the curtains have an interesting open-weave texture.

The modern living room (top right) walls and units are painted a rich Mediterranean blue — providing a perfect background for the books, painting and *objects d'art* — the colour contrast to the furniture and flooring is a particularly happy choice. The scheme makes a small box-like room appear much more interesting.

The feminine bedroom (top left) has a simple striped wall-paper in tones of pink on the bedhead wall, other walls and woodwork are white and the carpet is pale grey-green. The quilt cover, bed valance and pillow case echo these colours and bring the scheme to life.

The warm orange bedroom (see above), with natural wood wall and furniture could look rather overpowering, but the really bold quilt cover, contrasted with a plain valance, proves just how effective the use of pattern and plain can be

What do you mean by Texture?

Texture is difficult to describe, for although it is something you can see, it is also something you can feel—the rough, smooth, dull, shiny, translucent or velvety effect of a surface, this is texture, but so also is sunlight, filtering through louvres or open weave fabric. Just as a good colour scheme needs a certain amount of contrast to show it off, and just as a room should have an interesting mixture of pattern and plain, so the ideal room needs a contrast of textures.

The softer textures — shaggy-pile carpets, velvet upholstery, silk or satin drapes, flock wall-coverings, all give a warm, luxurious look to a room, while the smooth, shiny textures — glass-topped tables, leather upholstery, laminated plastic, chrome furniture, coarse open-weave curtain fabrics, foil wall-coverings, all give a cool rather harsh effect. So if you want a cosy, inviting room choose from the range of soft textures — if you want a modern, rather austere room, then select more from the smooth, shiny range. However if you want a well balanced scheme, you will need to introduce some contrasting textures. For example, if you have a very traditional dining room with a velvet-pile Wilton carpet, slubbed silk curtains, polished mahogany furniture, then you need to bring in something fairly harsh and shiny to complete the scheme—brass curtain poles and gilt picture frames would be ideal. On the other hand, if your room is very modern with rough hessian-textured walls, shiny chrome and glass furniture, windows screened with blinds, then have a shaggy-pile carpet.

The hall (top left) shows how texture interest can be added to a scheme even if the walls are to be painted. There are special 'relief' wallcoverings available (some in panel form, others which can be hung like wallpaper), specifically intended for over-painting. They are ideal for walls with poor surfaces, and once they are hung, can be painted every time you want to change the colour scheme, or 'freshen up' the existing one. The natural wood door, off-white Indian carpet and gilt picture frame all introduce different textures into the scheme.

The sitting room (bottom left) with matt-painted walls relies on the floorcovering and soft furnishings to provide texture contrast. The carpet tiles have a shaggy pile, the suite is upholstered in Dralon velvet, the cushions are slubbed silk, and the curtain fabric is open-weave allowing the light to filter through (and at the same time provides pattern interest). The accessories are well chosen too — the steel frame to the picture, steel track for the spotlights and glass top to the table emphasize the softness of the other textures.

In a bathroom setting (top right), tiles, mirrors and sanitaryware all provide harsh, shiny texture. Here the long-pile washable cotton fitted carpet and delicate filigree window screen and lampshade add an attractive softness to the scheme.

These two dining rooms (bottom right) are completely different in every way, yet contrasting textures have been used with equal skill in each room. The cool, austere, modern room has matt-painted walls, shiny painted woodwork, stark modern chrome and glass furniture — softer touches are provided by the cane seats, delicate glassware and table linen. In the traditional dining room with flock wallcovering, satin curtains and velvet upholstery, the chandelier and gilt picture frames provide texture contrast.

'Natural' Textures

Many interesting textures can also be provided by 'natural' items such as brick or stone-faced walls; marble, stone or slate fireplaces; polished wood floors; cork used for flooring or wallcovering; sisal carpeting and rush matting; cane and rattan; wood cladding and furniture; undyed wool used for carpets, tweed upholstery and drapes; leather upholstery; hessian wallcovering . . . All these 'natural' textures can blend with both modern and traditional schemes but should not be overdone — a room with one natural brick wall, another clad with wood, a stone fireplace, the remaining walls covered with hessian, a cork floor, pine furniture, tweed upholstery etc., would be rather overpowering, as though one were living in a room in an ecological museum!

The natural texture of marble and stone used in these two fireplaces illustrated show how important it is to choose the texture of the focal point of a room (as the fireplace generally is) very carefully. Marble tends to look very cool and elegant and needs a traditional scheme with some rich textures to set it off to advantage. Stone fireplaces, particularly the random-type, look much less severe and are more at home in a modern setting with long-pile carpet or rugs, tweed upholstery, open weave drapes and hessian wallcovering.

Although this picture (above right) is an outdoor one it is a perfect example of harmonising natural textures. The brick wall, even though it has been painted, still retains its own particular texture, the shiny gloss finish to

In this modern room setting (above right), the natural texture of wood (for wall cladding and furniture) has been skilfully combined with canvas and chrome furniture, exotic indoor plants and a three-tone carpet with 'sculptured' pile.

In this bathroom setting (below left), cork has been used as a wallcovering. This gives a lovely warm look to a room and helps to soften the rather stark texture of the richly-coloured sanitaryware. Indoor plants and dried flowers have both been used to advantage. The vinyl floorcovering looks like ceramic tiles and has been used as a splash-back on one wall.

the door contrasts with it, the wood barrel and rattan basket provide more natural textures and the whole is softened by the plants and fruit — the result is as pleasing as an Old Master painting. To translate this look into a room scheme you could have a natural brick wall, polish-ed wood floor with long-pile rug, cane furniture and lots of indoor plants.

A perfect contrast in textures (above) — the elegant marble-effect flooring (in fact a sheet vinyl), stoneware vase and dried flowers and grasses show each other off to advantage.

To Sum Up!

These six pictures prove more eloquently than any words, all the points I have been making on choosing colour schemes; mixing pattern and plain surfaces; selecting suitable, contrasting textures; adding those extra little accents and finishing touches to give the room that final special look. All the pictures are of the same bathroom, yet they look completely different — each room has its own atmosphere and personality. The starting point for each scheme was the patterned sheet-vinyl floor-covering — in some schemes this is predominant, but in others the flooring appears to fade into the background.

The first bathroom, in soft shades of grey-green and white is cool, elegant, feminine — the type of bathroom you might expect to find in a flat belonging to a business girl, or possibly the bathroom leading off the main bedroom in the Town house of a successful young couple! Pattern and plain surfaces have been subtly blended to create a restful scheme and the fluffy feathers, diaphanous white drapes and luxurious plants all soften what otherwise might have been a rather stark room.

The second bathroom obviously belongs to a bachelor! The colour scheme is a contrasting one in terracotta and blue, based on the classic Italian-style flooring and is very masculine — so is the leather texture of the stool and the simple, practical window treatment. Pictures, mirrors, etc., all echo the theme.

The third bathroom is very soft and feminine — the warm colour scheme of aubergine, pink and white is subtle and blends perfectly with the floor-covering. This could well be the bathroom in an old country house, which is used and enjoyed by all the family. Some of

the accessories are particularly unusual — the cane towel 'horse', cane overmantel used above the basin to hold bathroom jars and the converted piano stool with its *broderie anglaise* frill all add texture interest. The window has a louvred screen plus a roller blind.

The fourth bathroom (far right) has an oriental feel to it, yet could well be in a modern estate-built house. The choice of sharp green as the main colour might have been rather cold, but the brilliant ochre yellow accents give the scheme warmth and a really vibrant quality. The pattern on the flooring is very strong and is echoed in the yellow and white geometric design on the blind, and in the shape of the mirror and cluster of small pictures. Good mornings would definitely begin with a song in this room!

The fifth bathroom (below right) has a classical simplicity of design — it could well belong

to an Italian Count.

Brown tones from chocolate, through coffee to soft beige are cleverly mixed to create an atmosphere of warmth and richness, without detracting from the clear-cut design of the

flooring. The Victorian mahogany mirror, simple bentwood stool, beautifully fringed blind and marquetry pictures all help to enhance the scheme.

The sixth bathroom (above) is frankly opulent; the peaches-and-cream colour scheme, the satin curtains, ostrich feathers, Bauhaus-style mirror, pictures, light fittings and accessories all suggest the room belonged to a Hollywood star such as Jean Harlow, but is up-to-date as it can be for followers of the 1930's revival.

White Elephants!

So far the suggestions on planning, colour scheming, mixing pattern and plain and combining contrasting textures have more or less assumed you are starting to decorate and furnish a room completely from scratch, but very few people can actually do this – all too often there is an integration problem! In Chapter 1 (page 8–11) you will find help with fitting existing furniture into your room plan and in Chapter 2 (pages 16, 17) suggestions on adding colour samples of things you already have to your colour board, but very often the entire new scheme has to be fitted round a very predominant 'white elephant'! It may be a patterned carpet (or other floor covering); a three-piece suite; curtains; bathroom fittings or tiles; kitchen units . . . Whichever it is, take a long, hard look at the existing item and try to see it with fresh eyes – pretend it is a new purchase and this is the first time you are using it as a basis for a colour scheme.

If you are starting with a patterned carpet for example, it is possible to plan tone-on-tone schemes or contrasting ones based on the combination of colours in the carpet (see overleaf). A three-piece suite is usually less of a problem, since it can be re-upholstered (at a price) and there is always the possibility of loose covers or stretch covers in a colour to blend with the new scheme, but this type of furniture can be bulky and heavy-looking or even the wrong size and shape to fit into the planned new decor. One way of making a suite look less important is to have a carpet in the same colour, so it appears to 'melt into the landscape', or try setting it on a patterned or two-tone carpet and covering one chair in a contrasting colour. Coloured bathroom suites and tiles, laminated kitchen cupboards, work surfaces and tiles, can all be much more difficult to cope with, but there are ways of covering up tiles (see page 50), and it is surprising how many different colour schemes can be worked round a coloured bathroom suite or kitchen worktop.

Whichever 'white elephant' you have, don't forget to take a sample of the colour of the existing item with you when you shop – if you can't take an actual piece of carpet, fabric, tile, etc. then match to pieces of wool, embroidery silks or paint manufacturer's colour chips (see pages 14 and 15).

A suite can be given an entirely new look with a set of loose covers, stretch covers or different upholstery. In the **before** picture, the fairly bulky brown suite links with the patterned carpet — other colours in the carpet have been used to complete the room scheme.

After (top right) shows an entire colour change, with patterned covers on the suite and a new plain carpet.

After (centre right) is a less costly way of dealing with the problem. The same carpet remains, but the settee and one chair have been given stretch covers in deep gold to echo this colour in the carpet, and the second chair has a cover in the same fabric, but in tangerine-orange, which again picks out a colour in the carpet. New curtains, to tone, complete the scheme.

After (bottom right) is the most expensive conversion — a new carpet has been laid and the suite is recovered in a slightly paler tone than the carpet; an ideal way of making rather bulky furniture look less large, since it merges into the background.

How do I plan a Scheme Round my Patterned Carpet?

Planning a scheme round a patterned carpet may present problems since the carpet can last a long time and outlive several different schemes — possibly even several different locations!

Try to base the scheme on two or three colours in the carpet, keeping to plain surfaces with interesting textures (see Chapter 3). The really rich, warm, inviting traditional sitting room above is a tone-on-tone scheme which has been planned specifically round the colours in the carpet. The walls are painted a matt bronze-gold, the curtains are a deeper shade of bronze-olive velvet and the same fabric has been used to upholster the spoon-back chair. The deep brown leather Chesterfield has cushions in gold, tan and burnt-orange velvet and silk. The side-table (picked up at a jumble sale with a damaged top) is covered with a 'skirt' in deep gold. Touches of gilt (in picture frames and brass lamps, curtain

fabric, over white venetian blinds, allow light to filter into the room softly and the accessories in gold, turquoise, peacock, coral and white add dramatic pools of colour.

Later on you may decide on a change of carpet for the living room, but if the existing one is still good, it may be possible to have it cleaned, cut down (if necessary) and relaid in a smaller room. Below right we show the same carpet used in a bedroom with a bold hessian in deep red on the bedhead wall and plain emulsion on the other walls. A patchwork bedcover picks up all the colours in the carpet and a contrasting emerald green is used for curtains and bedside lampshades. The ceiling and most of the woodwork is white, but the doors of the fitted cupboards and door to the room are honey-beige to link with the rich gold tones in the original carpet.

pole, fender, desk accessories), give life to the scheme and help to add to the traditional atmosphere.

If you take the carpet with you when you move to a brand new house, or if you want to have modern decor, you can simply create a completely different atmosphere using the same carpet. Try a contrasting colour scheme for a change. In the drawing (above) three walls have been painted pale turquoise, one wall papered in a brown, peacock, gold and white striped paper, and the ceiling and woodwork picked out in white. The brown Chesterfield has been retained but new modern chairs, upholstered in golden-brown tweed have been added. The other furniture has been used elsewhere in the house, and a long white coffee table and white wall units give added life to the scheme. Curtains in a sheer beige and white

Kitchen Worksurfaces and Bathroom Suites

Once you have replanned your kitchen and bought new units, the chances are you will have to keep them for a long time, consequently it is practical to choose colours which are easy to live with. Very bright colours or strong patterns on worksurfaces should be avoided since they can become quite dazzling and tiring on the eyes after preparing food on them for only a short while. Painted units are easier to change, but those which have a special spray-painted finish or are faced with a plastic laminate are much harder to alter, so again it is wise to choose an unobtrusive pattern or an adaptable colour. There are ways of giving units an up-to-date look (see the pictures) but laminated plastic worktops cannot be successfully painted or

covered — the only way to make a colour change is to replace them!

Coloured bathroom suites are often considered to be the ultimate luxury, but before making a final decision remember you will probably need to change your colour scheme 4 or 5 times and will have to base each new scheme on the same colour suite. It is surprising just how adaptable a 'clinical' white one can be (see the six schemes on pages 42 and 43), but if you have already got coloured bathroom equipment you may be able to 'ring the changes' with a surprising number of colour schemes. Tile treatment is another matter again, turn over the page for help with this problem.

In this kitchen (top left) the units were the 'paintable white-

space was painted Tango.

For those who don't fancy painting stripes or patterns on their units there is an alternative! A self-adhesive plastic which can be bought by the yard is ideal for a quick cover-up. Many of these come in mix-and-match ranges, as can be seen from the two pictures (left and below). The blue kitchen has a patch-work-effect splashback and the cupboard doors have been covered in two different tones of blue self-adhesive plastic.

The warm brown and orange kitchen was given a new lease of life with a smart geometric self-stick vinyl — the neat, smaller version of the design goes on the wall, the bolder 'companion' design is used on the cupboards in cut-out form. The stool and other accessories were added — the colours and design chosen to enhance the new decoration scheme.

A similar effect could be achieved with decorative trans-fers, which are now available in a wide range of colours and designs. Some are self-stick but for a more permanent result, use the waterslide type.

wood type and worktops luckily were white. The previous scheme was based on red, sunshine yellow and white, but a rich autumnal effect was created entirely by the clever use of paint. Three colours — Tango orange, Seagull grey and Scorched Earth brown give the room a really modern look. Most of the wall cupboards and drawer fronts were painted brown, and all the base unit doors were painted in the pale grey. The orange and brown paint were then used to decorate the doors with semi-circles, and one base unit and top cupboard were 'striped' in the three colours (first painted grey and the brown and orange stripes painted in afterwards). The stripes were continued on the area of wall behind, and the remaining wall

Tiled Surfaces

In the kitchen and bathroom one of the main problems is trying to hide tiles which are either old, ugly and even 'crazed', or of the wrong colour to fit into a new scheme. Retiling is a rather drastic answer and often not practical, particularly if you live in rented property. If you *do* decide to remove old tiles, you may well find the plaster behind comes away with the tile and will need 'making good' — small holes, cracks and bumps can be coped with by the do-it-your-selfer, but really bad damage to plaster will need replastering professionally. It is possible, of course, to cover up a bad wall

with wood cladding, and since this is fixed to the wall by means of battens, the wall underneath does not need to be very smooth! Plastic laminates can also be fixed to the wall by this method, or stuck directly onto the surface (so long as it is reasonably flat) by means of an impact adhesive, so either alternative is worth considering.

On the other hand, if you cannot face the thought of the work and mess involved in actually removing the old tiles, there are several ways of covering, or partially covering them up so you are able to plan a new colour scheme without being too tied by the existing items.

Wood-cladding was the answer in this problem kitchen (above). The old tiles were not even removed, battens were fixed to the walls and horizontal tongue and groove boards used to clad the entire area of wall, and carried up onto the sloping ceiling.

In this bathroom (far left) the latest textured wallcovering has been used — this is an embossed vinyl which gives walls the beautiful sculptured look of tiles at a fraction of the cost — and a fraction of the work too! It can be used on bath panels, on shelves and window sills so the room can have a fully 'integrated' look. It is practical in rooms with a condensation problem, since the surface is soft and warm to the touch. When you want to change the scheme, the wall-covering strips off easily leaving a ready 'lined' wall which you can redecorate to your own taste and requirements.

Tile 'cover-ups' (above left) are the answer when your problem is one of 'crazed' or simply wrong-colour tiles. Several manufacturers make these in a range of different designs, colours and size. They are all extremely easy to apply, being self-adhesive, they peel off the backing sheet and are easy to smooth into position. You can stick them on every tile (as in the kitchen picture) to form a specific geometric design, or at random, whichever you prefer.

In the kitchens (see below), where the problem is a 'splash back' tiled in the wrong colour, or where there are very old tiles you can stick new, slim, metal tiles over the top and completely cover them.

Can I Dye It?

If you are dying for a change of colour scheme but can't afford to buy any major items you may be surprised to learn it is possible to dye almost anything! Of course you can't dye a dark colour lighter, unless you are able to strip out all the old colour and start from scratch, but it is possible to do even this with some things like curtains, bed-covers and linen. Carpets and loose-covers can be success-fully dyed at home, and also there are some professional ser-vices who undertake this work if you prefer not to try and tackle the job yourself.

Before: This living room had an off-white wool carpet which

was beginning to look dingy, a brown suite, coffee-coloured walls, beige curtains and accessories were in tones of orange and turquoise. A new suite was a sudden bargain buy at sale time, and although blue and browns can look lovely together, somehow the pale blue looked wrong on the off-white carpet — the answer was to base the scheme on blues and greens.

After: First the walls, woodwork and ceiling were repainted white and the net Terylene curtains were freshened up with Curtain White. Next the carpet was dyed with Moss Green carpet dye, the curtains and some of the cushion covers were dyed rich Arabian Blue. A remnant of fabric, also picked up cheaply at sale time, was dyed Leaf Green and used to make cushions and a lampshade. To complete the scheme, a rather tired-looking white table cloth and napkins were dyed to match the curtains and a Batik wall-hanging was made from white lawn dyed blue and green — even the dried grasses underwent a change of colour, via the dye pot!

The bedroom **before** had been decorated to tone with the cane headboard and was looking frankly a little dull. The wallpaper needed changing as this had become grubby (especially where it was used on the panels of the cupboards), the carpet needed freshening up, particularly inside the bedroom door where the colour from the landing carpet tended to 'bleed' into it.

The **after** shows just what can be done with dye — the carpet was dyed Scarlet, the bed linen Tahiti Rose and blanket Scarlet. The walls, cupboard frames and chest were painted white and panels for the cupboards, bedhead wall and lampshade were tie-dyed using Tahiti Rose and Mexican Red. The natural cane bedhead looked wrong with this new scheme so even this was dyed red with a new wood dye.

Turn over for details on how to dye . . .

53

How do I Dye It?

Most fabrics and carpets can be dyed, but first get to know your fibres! Since there are several different types of dye available, and two basic methods of dyeing fabric, it is essential to identify the fibres in your fabrics. If you have no idea (labels on things often give fibre content) you can send a cutting to the dye manufacturer's consumer advisory service, but remember if a material is washable, then more often than not, it's dyeable too. Consult the chart for the type of dye to use and start with a clean carpet or fabric — there is no point in dyeing dirt!

To Colour a Carpet

Most carpets in wool, nylon, Evlan, and mixtures of any of these fibres or mixtures with acrylics such as Courtelle can by dyed, but *not* if the carpet is foam backed, very shaggy-piled or composed of only Acrylic fibres (again the label should tell you your carpet 'mix').

Remove all the furniture from the room and then vacuum the carpet thoroughly. Shampoo if necessary, taking great care to remove any stains as these could show through the dye. When the carpet is clean, protect the skirtings (or surrounding floor area) from splashes with newspaper. Dissolve the dye in boiling water, following the manufacturer's instructions, and make sure you make up enough dye for the entire carpet — one container dyes 4–6 sq. yards (approx. 5 sq. m). For the best results, keep the solution simmering on the stove, transferring small quantities to another bowl as needed. Work the hot dye well into the pile with a fairly stiff brush (a soft-bristled scrubbing brush is ideal) as quickly as possible, taking care to dye all the pile but *not* to saturate the carpet. If the carpet is partly faded, dye these areas first and then go over the entire carpet again. If you have to stop before finishing the carpet, break off in a zig-zag rather than a hard straight line. *Note*. Remember to start in the corner furthest away from the door and work towards your way out! Shut the door on the room when you have finished and leave the carpet to dry thoroughly — a period from 24–48 hours depending on how wet you have made the carpet and how warm and well ventilated the room is. When the newly dyed carpet is *completely dry*, vacuum it and replace the furniture.

You can dye a plain carpet to make it look patterned — bold stripes, geometrics, sophisticated *Art Deco* . . . mark out the areas before dyeing or use a stencil. A patterned carpet *can* be dyed, but it won't look plain, however it will look different — base your choice of colour on the pattern's strongest colour and the effect will be of a tone-on-tone carpet.

To Refresh Curtains

Tired white nets can be given a new lease of life in two ways — they can be freshened up by washing in hot water with a special Curtain White (as in our living room on the previous page) or they can be dyed a completely different colour. The type of dye you use for this will again depend on whether they are made from cotton, Terylene or other synthetic fibre net so look at the fibres chart before you start. Heavier curtains are best dyed in the washing machine, using a dye specially created for the purpose, but in order to allow freedom of movement, so the colour penetrates evenly, only dye half the machine's normal wash-load. Remove any lining so the curtains will be less bulky. If you don't have your own washing machine you can wash-and-dye in some launderettes so long as you consult the attendant and leave the machine clean afterwards.

First strip out the existing colour (if possible) with Dygon, particularly if the curtains have faded, to bring them back to a level base colour — this can also be done in the washing machine. Then dye to the colour of your choice using one pack of 2 lbs (1·25 kg) *dry* fabric — that is about 10 sq. yds (9–10 sq. m) medium-weight fabric — see the weight chart. If you can't use a washing machine, then you can dye curtains with a cold dye in the bath, but remember they will be very heavy when wet so you may need help with handling them.

Linen

Table and bed linen, including blankets are also fun to dye — again the washing machine process is the most successful and you will have to dye according to fabric type. Wool blankets as well as other fibre blankets can be dyed in the machine so long as you remove any stains and then wet the blanket thoroughly first. Use the normal blanket wash cycle making sure the blanket can really move freely in the machine so the dye penetrates. Dyeing a blanket in the bath is possible, but again it is very difficult to handle when wet because of the weight.

APPROXIMATE WEIGHT GUIDE
Do Not Dye more than half machine's maximum wash load

Candlewick Bedspreads	(Single)	1/1·75 g	(2-3½ lb)
	(Double)	1·75/3·5 kg	(3½-7 lb)
Curtains	(1 pair long, heavy-weight)	3·5 kg	(7 lb)
	(1 pair long, medium-weight)	1/1·5 kg	(2-3 lb)
Chair Covers	(Cretonne or linen, light-weight)	1/1·5 kg	(2-3 lb)
	(Cretonne or linen, heavy-weight)	1·75/2·5 kg	(3½-5 lb)
Bath Mats	(Towelling)	500/750 g	(1-1¼ lb)
	(Tumble Twist)	1/1·5 kg	(2-3 lb)
Tablecloths	(Heavy-weight plush)	1/1·5 kg	(2-3 lb)
	(Damask or linen)	500/750 g	(1-1¼ lb)
Blankets	(Single)	1·25/2 kg	(2¼-4 lb)
	(Double)	1·75/3·5 kg	(3½-7 lb)

Choose The Right Dye For Your Fabric

1 Multi Purpose Dye — 47 colours, 1 tin dyes ½ lb (250 g) dry fabric, 2-3 sq. yd./sq. m. medium weight fabric

2 Liquid Dye — 18 colours, 1 bottle dyes 2 lb (1 kg) dry fabric, 8-10 sq. yd./sq. m. medium weight fabric

3 Wash 'n Dye — 18 colours, 1 pack dyes 2½ lb (1·25 kg) dry fabric, 10 sq. yd./sq. m. medium weight fabric

4 Cold Dye — 25 colours in small tins; 12 colours in plastic drums
1 tin dyes ½ lb (250 g) dry fabric,
2-3 sq. yd./sq. m. medium weight fabric
1 drum dyes 2½ lb (1·25 kg) dry fabric,
10 sq. yd./sq.m. medium weight fabric
Use with Cold Dye Fix

Natural Fabrics
1 2 3 4 Canvas
1 2 3 4 Cotton
1 2 3 4 Hessian
1 2 3 4 Linen
1 2 3 4 Silk
1 2 3 4 Wool

Acetates and Triacetates
1 2 3 Acetate
1 2 3 Dicel
1 2 3 Lancofil
1 2 3 Lancola
1 2 3 Lancolene
1 2 3 Lansil
1 2 3 Tricel
1 2 3 Tricelon

Nylons and Nylon Mixtures
1 2 3 Banlon
1 2 3 Bri-nylon Lycra
1 2 3 Celon
1 2 3 Enkalon
1 2 3 Helanca
1 2 3 Nylon wool
1 2 3 Perlon
1 2 3 Tendrelle

Polyesters and Polyester mixtures
1 2 4 Crimplene cotton
1 2 4 Dacron cotton
1 2 4 Diolen cotton
1 2 — Tergal
1 2 4 Terylene cotton
1 2 4 Trevira cotton

Viscose Rayons and Rayon Mixtures
1 2 3 4 Darelle
1 2 3 4 Delustra
1 2 3 4 Evlan cotton
1 2 3 4 Raycelon nylon
1 2 3 4 Sarille Terylene
1 2 3 4 Vincel cotton
1 2 3 4 Viscose Rayon cotton

Acrylics – Don't Dye
Acrilan
Cashmilon
Courtelle
Dralon
Leacril
Neo-spun
Orlon
Sayelle

I've got a Problem!

Sloping ceilings, in attic rooms, dormer rooms *and* modern chalet bungalows, can present decoration problems too. But there are ways of making even the tiniest room look twice as large, and it is not always done with mirrors! Space is always at a premium, so it often makes sense to have dual-purpose rooms, but this can create planning and furnishing problems (more about making space in Chapter 8), and children's rooms should be flexible too. This chapter sets out to help with some of these problems.

Planning colour schemes and decoration, combining existing items with new schemes, mixing pattern with plain, choosing contrasting textures — these are not the only things to consider when homemaking. There are many other problems which crop up and, more often than not, they are problems of proportion. Halls in particular can be difficult to decorate and a large, high-ceilinged room in an older house may have looked marvellous in its heyday with marble fireplace, complete with overmantel, heavy over-stuffed upholstery, large ornate pieces of furniture, and elaborately draped pelmets and curtains. But once you remove the overmantel and fill the room with smaller items of furniture, screen the windows with a simpler style of curtain, the tall proportions of the room can seem very cold and unfriendly. There are ways of making such ceilings seem less high, without going to the expense of putting in a false ceiling (which often spoils the proportions of the room anyway!).

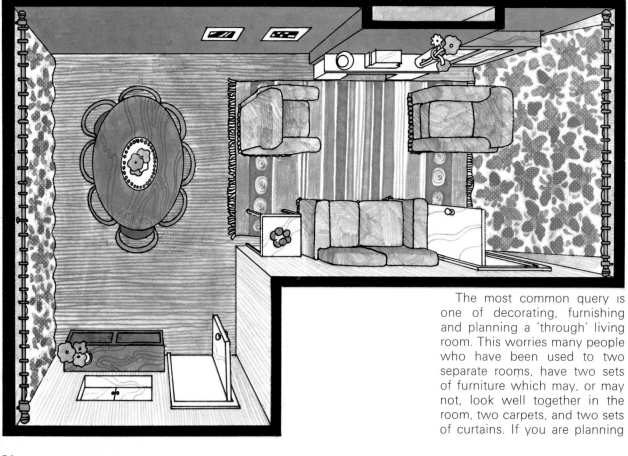

The most common query is one of decorating, furnishing and planning a 'through' living room. This worries many people who have been used to two separate rooms, have two sets of furniture which may, or may not, look well together in the room, two carpets, and two sets of curtains. If you are planning

vinyl over the whole area and then use one of your carpets as a 'square' in the sitting area. Decorate most of the walls the same way, but if the room is long and narrow, the end wall could be painted a rich colour or papered with a bold design (see page 28), or if it is L-shaped you might prefer to treat the long fireplace wall differently from the others. Curtains should be the same at both ends of the room, so try to get new ones to blend with the scheme. If you really do have to make do with one existing set of curtains, link them with the scheme in a positive way.

In the green and cream 'through' living room (top left), which is divided by a sliding door, the carpet is rich cream throughout. The majority of the walls have a geometric designed wallcovering in shades of green and cream, with one wall painted a rich, dark green. The upholstered furniture is in cream with green base and the wood furniture is stained green.

The drawing (far left) shows how to carry colours from one area to the other when the room is L-shaped. The long wall, common to both areas of the room is covered in rose-coloured hessian, while the other walls have a simple textured-stripe wallcovering. A grey cord carpet covers the floor, but a carpet 'square' in turquoise, peacock and rose softens the sitting area floor. Curtains at both ends of the room are patterned in tones of pinks, turquoise, grey and white.

to make the structural change yourself, you have probably allowed for certain new purchases in your budget, but suppose the living/dining room is in a new house and you have to marry together some of your existing furniture and furnishings in one room.

The golden rule is to try and 'zone' the two areas so they seem separate, without necessarily putting up room dividers. It is important to aim for colour continuity, so try to have the same floorcovering throughout. If you can't afford to carpet, then you could lay a sheet of

This dining room with hall beyond (below left) is a typical example of many older-style houses. Here the rich gold has been used to lead the eye from room to room, creating a feeling of continuity.

Coping with a Slope

Some attic rooms in old houses have sloping ceilings but so do many modern chalet bungalows, and if you open up a room in the roof you are bound to have at least two areas of sloping ceiling. The dormer window can be another problem in this type of room since it can be difficult to curtain and it so often cuts the light to a minimum. Much the most attractive way of decorating a bedroom with this type of architectural feature is to use a pretty floral wall-covering on the walls *and* the sloping part of the ceiling. The flat part can be painted a plain toning colour.

In this attic bedroom (above) the scheme is cool and restful and only a net curtain screens the window because the window is not overlooked. If you prefer paint to paper then adapt the scheme by painting the sloping ceiling and walls in a fairly strong colour, with the flat ceiling and walls in white. Use patterned fabrics for bedcover

and curtains.

If you want to make the most of all available space, the area under a dormer window must not be wasted. If the dormer is in a living room (many flats in converted houses have this problem) then put a desk under the window (bottom left) — if the room is a bedroom, use this position for the dressing table, or in a child's room for a desk or play surface. Make two-tier café style curtains for the window and paint the area of the dormer and the flat ceiling white with the sloping area in a rich colour.

Some sloping windows simply will not take curtains at all — in the opened-up loft (above right) which is used as a teen-age 'den' the walls are painted

'Elixir' orange, the sloping ceiling and woodwork in 'Hessian' beige to match the upholstery and gay patchwork-effect blinds in orange, beige, brown, coffee and white screen the window. This fabric is also used for fitted divan cover and cushions.

In a Victorian house, where

the deep-set dormer may well be arched, crisp frilled nets screen the window, following the curve of the arch (they have to be pinned or stapled into position), paint the area round the window white to give maximum reflected light, and use a pastel colour for sloping ceiling *and* walls (above).

I've got a Problem Hall!

Halls can be difficult to decorate since they are often
large, cold and unfriendly areas
with high ceilings and long
'drops' of wall to be papered —
difficult to cope with physically,
quite apart from choosing the
colour scheme. Alternatively the
problem may be quite the opposite — the hall is so tiny, it gives
a cramped feel to the whole
house, but it is possible to
create an impression of space
(see Chapter 8). Consequently
the hall tends to be a rather
neglected area, being redecor-
ated less frequently than the
rest of the house, even though
it is the first part of the home
seen by visitors!

The hall can also be so much
wasted space, so it may be
worth considering making more
use of it, or removing part of a
wall to make an open-plan area
(see pages 12 and 13).

Another important thing to
consider when decorating the
hall, stairs and landing is that
all rooms lead off from them,
so colour schemes should be
co-ordinated whenever possible
(more about this on pages 84
and 85).

This large hall (top right),
with its high ceiling, has been
decorated in a distinctive style.
The walls are covered with a
bold traditional design in ready-
pasted vinyl, and the ceiling,
which was in a bad condition
was papered with a heavily embossed Anaglypta and then emul-
sioned with rich Saffron gold
paint. This echoes the carpet
colour, making floor and ceiling
appear closer together — the
treatment of the arch and cornice
helps further to visually create an
impression of less height.

The meandering rather gloomy
hall (below right) in a 'mansion'
flat was an awkward shape and
seemed to be all doors. The
answer was to use a pretty, but
not too bold wallcovering in
shades of olive, orange and
white, on all walls. The ceiling
was painted white to give maximum reflected light, and woodwork, including all the doors,
was painted olive to tone with
the carpet — a very large mirror,
set into a recess, gives the
illusion of greater space and
disguises a 'blind' corner.

A long narrow hall (centre
right) in a modern flat has a
warm welcoming atmosphere.
The ceiling is painted red, to
tone with the table and accessories, and the double door at
the end of the hall has been

painted white with a black frame
and then decorated with self-
adhesive plastic in a bold geometric pattern.

It can all be done with
mirrors! A small pokey hall (far
right) in an old terraced house

looks twice as large because one wall has been covered with mirror glass.

If a hall is fairly large (below), with an understair cupboard, it may be possible to take away the cupboard, store cleaning things in the kitchen, and convert the area under the stairs into a mini-study or sewing/hobbies corner. *Note:* Make sure the boarding of the cupboard does not support the stairs!

Giving a Dull Room Individuality

Small or box-like rooms can be completely transformed by an old technique known as *trompe l'oeil* or 'eye deceivers'. In many a stately home, an entrance appears to have magnificent marble pillars, but in fact the walls are painted to look as though the marble columns stand out. Friezes and even ceilings were also painted to look as though they were in relief, like the classical ones in Greece and Rome — again examples of the decorator's art. There is no reason why these ideas should not be adapted to the humblest home. Nowadays the vogue for painting wallpatterns is growing, and you can make the design as simple or complicated as you like depending on inclination and artistic ability.

Here are some helpful hints:

1. Start by sketching wallpattern, to scale, on a piece of squared paper. Divide up the wall accordingly.

2. When a straight line is required, rule a line in pencil first and then apply decorator's masking tape. To achieve a straight vertical line use a plumb line (available from do-it-yourself and decoration shops).

3. Use a thin brush for pattern outlines and fill in with a larger brush. Alternatively use paint pads.

4. When sketching a pattern featuring a right angle use a set square.

5. Before sketching a pattern, first paint the entire area white. This provides a good base and may avoid the necessity for two coats of colour.

6. If attempting a freehand design, sketch the outlines first in chalk directly on to the wall.

7. Use a quick drying paint such as emulsion or vinyl.

8. If using several colours start with the lightest first and work from top to bottom.

A similar technique can be used to paint friezes round a wall to make it seem less tall — an easy way is to cut out a stencil in really stiff card or hardboard and paint through this.

Note. If you don't have the courage to try painting patterns and friezes, then you can cheat with a 'photowall' which is hung just like wallpaper, but it has a view or vista on it — or cover a door (at the end of a corridor for example) with a door poster depicting a sunset or moonlight on water. Friezes too can be cut out from wallpaper or vinyl with a definite motif and stuck round a wall.

An easy wallpattern looks like a simple landscape with the red sun going down in the West! This was sketched onto the wall with chalk. The blue sky was painted first, leaving the white patch for the cloud, then each colour area was filled in separately, working from top to bottom. Each area was left until touch dry (30 minutes — 1 hour) before painting the adjacent section. This treatment would look equally effective over one wall.

These two wallpatterns are much more complicated. In the bathroom the landscape effect has been carried onto the bath panel and the whole painted area reflected in a wall of mirror. In the grey-blue room even the door seems to disappear on the crest of a wave. A similar technique to the one described

above was used for both rooms.

If you feel your drawing abilities are not quite up to creating a landscape in paint, then you can use a mural-effect produced for the purpose — designs range from mountain scenes to the woods in autumn, you can even find yourself in the middle of a winter scene painted by Breughel! These come in sections and are easy to hang. Special door posters are also available which would brighten up a dull corridor if they were stuck on every door.

How do I Plan and Decorate a Dual-purpose Room?

If you cannot manage to extend your house (see Chapter 8), but you simply must have more space, you may find one answer is to create a dual-purpose room, thereby releasing another room for a different purpose. As children grow up it may be possible to convert their bedroom to a bedsitting room, and the family living room might then become a dining room or study (if you have two 'reception' rooms). A separate dining room can double as a study, or even as a sewing and hobbies room if you invest in some built-in furniture. Con-

vertible settees used to be neither fish nor fowl — awkward to sit on, uncomfortable to sleep on and not exactly elegant to look at, but at last manufacturers have solved the problem and there are many really good-looking convertibles around. Consequently the sitting room can double as a guest room, or you might like to make your own bedroom into an upstairs sitting room, freeing downstairs

rooms for family living. The kitchen too, is often neglected as a possible dual-purpose room — large kitchens can do double duty as a playroom, so long as small children cannot be burnt or scalded!

A study-corner (above) made in the dining room — the chimney breast, desk shelf, bookshelves and filing drawers have the warm look of natural rosewood, but are actually faced with self-adhesive plastic. The desk shelf does double duty too, as a serving table when there are too many dishes for the dining table.

A more streamlined study area (left) at one end of the living room is used by its owner daily as an art studio. The drawing board can be slanted or flat and maximum use is made of the adjustable shelving system. Cork wall tiles are used as a practical pin board.

The richly-coloured 'with it' bedsitting room (right) belongs to a 15-year old girl who likes to ask her friends in to listen to records. The drawer divan doubles as a settee, and bedding is stored in one of the roomy drawers underneath leaving the other free for bulky sweaters. Large cushions give added comfort and the mattress is covered with a Kelim rug to match the flooring.

A very unusual bedsitting room is made in a chalet bungalow with sloping ceilings. The fabric, which matches the wallpaper is used for curtains which form a bed alcove — the bedcover and window curtains in matching fabric (above left).

The main bedroom in a three-bedroom house is converted to an upstairs bedsitting room where the adults can sit, leaving the downstairs open-plan living room as a family area. The streamlined storage units house all the clothes and the old fire-place was removed, making the shelf-desk space. The settee 'unfolds' to make a full-sized double bed (above right).

Planning and Decorating Rooms for Children

The most important thing to remember when planning a scheme for a child is that they quickly outgrow the 'kittens and bunnies' stage, so it is necessary

to plan a room which will 'grow with the child' thereby avoiding having to make expensive changes and new purchases every few years.

Most people want a pretty nursery to start with, but it is wise to decorate one wall only with a nursery paper or vinyl — use emulsion paint on the other walls (over a textured paper if preferred) so when you want to redecorate the room for a 4-year-old you can strip the one wall, and either repaint all the walls, paint three and re-paper one or paper all four. If plain curtains are chosen, these will blend with future schemes, or if you decide on patterned ones, do not choose expensive fabric — these can then be replaced with blinds or new curtains.

Furniture should be practical — easy to clean, preferably paintable or with a laminated finish. Try to buy from a range which is likely to last, so you can add to it as your child grows and the need for storage increases. Also choose practical floorcoverings as small children are notoriously messy, particularly if their bedroom has to be used as a playroom as well.

Our room which grows with the child demonstrates just how worth-while it is to plan ahead.

Stage One: In the first picture the room is ready for a new baby. A pretty nursery paper has been used on the sloping wall, with matching fabrics for curtains — the other walls are painted in a toning colour. A nursery screen has been made to match the curtains, to keep out the draught when the baby is being bathed or in the cot with the window open. The rocking chair is used as a nursing chair and the trolley takes all the items needed for changing and feeding a baby. The floor has easy-to-clean sheet vinyl, softened by a washable cotton rug. The crib will be changed for a cot when the baby is about 9 months old and at that stage some clothes storage will be added.

Stage Two: the room is now ready for a four-year old. Simple built-in cupboards have been added, with open fronts and roller blinds instead of doors — they match the blind at the window, which in turn matches the pretty floral patterned vinyl which has been hung on walls and ceiling. The 'grown-up' bed has a washable cotton cover in crocus yellow. The floor is the same as stage one, but the cotton rug has been taken into the bathroom where it is less likely to suffer paint 'spills'!

Stage Three: a complete change of colour scheme and the room is now a teenage 'bedsit', with cool green painted walls. A desk-cum-dressing table runs under the window with a laminated plastic top and pull-out chest — the chair folds down to give more floor space when needed. The bed base is made from filing drawers, which provide storage for papers, records etc., with a firm mattress on top. The Continental blanket doubles as a bedcover and scatter cushions make for comfortable lounging on bed or floor. The new blinds match the colour scheme and the floor has been covered with carpet tiles, laid in a definite design to echo the pattern on the blanket. Bookshelves, hi-fi and spotlights are all part of the teenage scene.

When possible children should have space to play, where they can make a mess without being nagged about it! In this room, *bottom left*, all the surfaces are washable and the walls and furniture have been decorated with cut-out motifs in self-adhesive plastic. The blackboard wall was made by nailing two horizontal strips of picture-frame beading across the wall and filling the gap with a dark-coloured self-adhesive plastic. This will be simple to remove and the wall can easily be re-decorated when a drawing surface is no longer needed.

Another way of creating flexible rooms for children, *bottom right*, is by building furniture on the same principle as a construction toy! Basically it is rather like builder's scaffolding, made from brightly-coloured tubes which are held together by a three-way clamp — two or three tubes are held together at right-angles to each other and locked tight by just one bolt. The system can be used to make bunks, ladders, slides, storage and play areas, and can be dismantled and altered to suit the needs of a growing family.

Choosing a Carpet

A carpet with a traditional design (below) is 100% Acrilan and woven by the Axminster method. Here it is laid throughout the ground floor and carried up the stairs and on to the landing. The furnishings and wall colours have been chosen to blend with the carpet.

Wool is used for this 'Berber' look carpet (right) in natural creamy tones. Plain Wilton is used for the steps and a hand-tufted wall-hanging rug looks well on a wall.

So much confusion exists concerning carpets, largely due to the extravagent claims made in advertisements! Up until fairly recently there were three basic types of fitted carpet — Wilton, Axminster and cord. These were all made from natural fibres, wool in the case of the Wilton and Axminster carpets, and animal hair or sisal for the cord. These carpets were hardwearing and most people bought a fairly expensive carpet for the areas of the home which got the most wear (living room, hall, stairs and landing) and expected it to last for about 30 years! The golden rule was 'spend as much as you can afford on your carpets since wear-ability can be directly related to cost'. However, in the last few years the situation has changed — tufted carpets were introduced about 20 years ago, and at first, since they were in the experimental stage, did not always live up to the promises made by the manufacturers — luckily they are now vastly improved. Tufteds were followed by the invention of carpet tiles, and all sorts of fibres and blends of fibres were developed for carpet manufacture. It is still wise to choose a hardwearing carpet for the areas of the home which get the most wear and through 'traffic', but this need not necessarily be the most expensive carpet available!

Wiltons and Axminsters are no longer always made entirely of wool, they can be a blend of wool with a synthetic fibre combining the natural resilience of wool with the easy cleaning properties of the synthetic, or they can be made entirely from a synthetic fibre. The words Wilton and Axminster in fact refer to the carpet *weave* and not to the carpet content. (More about weaves over the page). Tufted is also a method of carpet construction, and just to confuse the issue, this type of carpet is sometimes produced in wool as well as in other fibres and blends of fibres.

There are other confusing words in the carpet salesman's vocabulary: 'body', 'broadloom', 'square'. These refer to carpet widths. 'Body' means the carpet comes in strips of various widths, usually 27 ins (69 cm) or 36 ins (91 cm) wide by up to 50 yds

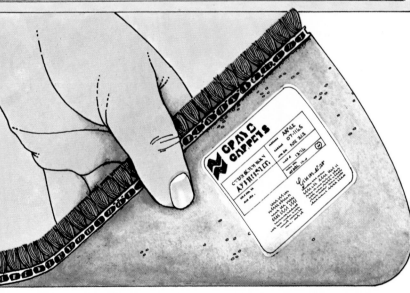

near to the standard width of the carpet; in some cases one or two strips of body can be added to the broadloom to completely close-cover the floor. Carpet squares are normally used on a polished wood floor or other hard surface surround, and can be turned round at intervals to even out the wear.

The main fibres used in carpet construction are wool, nylon, acrylic and rayon and can be used on their own or mixed in various proportions. They do not necessarily appear under the name nylon, acrylic or rayon, but have brand names such as Bri-nylon, Du Pont 501, Enkalon, Allyn 707 (nylon). Acrilan, Courtelle, Orlon Type 36 (acrylic). Fibro, Evlan, Evlan M (rayon/viscose). There are other fibres also being developed including polyester (Terylene) and polypropylene (Meraklon).

Wool has a natural resilience or springiness which allows wool carpets to maintain their good looks after a lot of hard wear, also it is warm and resists dirt, but make sure your wool carpet is mothproofed. Nylon is tougher, not so resilient and has a slightly shiny texture. It soils easily but is easily cleaned, and is often mixed with wool to give extra wear and cleanability. Acrylic is the man-made fibre which comes nearest to wool in looks and behaviour, it wears well but soils easily. Like nylon it is easy to clean. Rayon (Viscose) does not have the same resilience or hardwearing qualities so it is frequently mixed with other fibres to produce a cheaper carpet. All-rayon carpets should be used for relatively light wear (bedroom). Nowadays most carpets carry a label giving full details of weave, fibre mixture and type of use. The five classifications are: Light domestic e.g. bedroom use; Light to medium domestic use; Medium domestic or light contract use; Heavy domestic or medium contract use; Luxury domestic or heavy contract use.

(45·7 m) long although some staircarpet can be found in 18 inch (46 cm) and 22½ inch (57 cm) widths. 'Broadloom' is woven on a broad loom and comes in various widths, the most popular being 9 ft (274 cm), 12 ft (366 cm) and 15 ft (457 cm). A carpet 'square' need not be square, it can be oblong, and is really a rug which is properly finished at both ends. Body carpet is used for stairs, and also can be laid to close-cover odd-shaped rooms, but it has to be seamed which does not look very attractive in a large room. Broadloom can be cut to give fitted carpeting without joins where the room size is

Different Methods of Weaving Carpets

The three main methods of weaving conventional carpets are Axminster, Wilton and Tufted described fully below, although there are cords, which are manufactured in a similar manner to Wilton, but the uncut pile is looped tightly over the backing giving the characteristic self-striped appearance. Cord carpeting, like the other types of carpet, now comes in a wide range of fibres and blends of fibre. Cord made from animal hair, or a blend containing a good percentage of animal hair, sisal, or one of the hardwearing synthetics should be hardwearing, but is not usually regarded as a 'luxury' carpet, consequently it is not used as often as cut pile carpets for sitting rooms or living areas. There are also Needleloom felts, some of which are very hardwearing, non-woven 'compressed' carpets, as well as special developments with nylon. Hand-woven carpets and rugs, mainly Oriental, are also available, at a price, and if you are considering buying something like this, then always seek the advice of an expert since this is a specialist subject and a good purchase can be regarded as an investment.

Axminster Carpet is a woven carpet and all the fibre is in the pile and none hidden in the backing so it can be recognised by examining the underside — the pile is woven at the same time as the backing. There are two types of Axminster — Gripper and Spool. With the gripper method, the pattern is controlled by a jacquard which lifts the required colour to the correct height so that the gripper (it looks like a bird's beak) can grip the yarn and insert it in the backing. The process is normally limited to eight colours. With spool Axminster, the number of colours is unlimited, as they are pre-set on a spool and inserted into the backing yarns from a continuous chain. Axminster always has a cut pile.

Gripper Axminster

Spool Axminster

Wilton Carpet is usually plain, a tweedy tone-on-tone effect, or a very simple pattern — all colours used in the pile (usually restricted to 5) are woven into the backing, giving an almost built-in-cushion, the pile can be cut (called velvet) looped or twisted or even a mixture of cut and looped (called sculptured).

Wilton

Tufted Carpet is made in quite a different way — it is not woven, the tufts are individually inserted into a pre-woven backing, using equipment like a giant sewing machine. The back is then coated with a latex compound to anchor the tufts and a second backing is often added to give extra stability. The pile can be looped or cut.

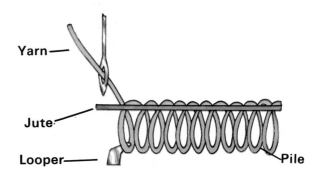

Yarn — Jute — Looper — Pile

Tufted

part of a special range where 24 designs, based on a palette of 60 different colours can really combine to give mix-and-match floorcoverings throughout home or hotel.

Far left: Another Wilton, this time striped in shades of beige and brown and woven from a blend of fibres — 80% wool and 20% nylon. This carpet, laid throughout the entire living room, hall, stairs and landing area of the house gives colour continuity, creating a feeling of spaciousness. Bedroom carpets could be in tones of plain brown and beige to link with the striped carpet. Striped carpets are ideal for narrow rooms if they are laid widthwise, since they then make the area look wider.

Below: This Tufted carpet has a shaggy pile and looks like an artist's impression of full-blown chrysanthemum heads — the overall effect is one of interesting texture rather than a bold pattern. The shaded effect is created by a sophisticated process which dyes each tuft from tip to root.

Top: Axminster carpet in tones of greens, gold, tan-orange and peacock in an 80% wool and 20% nylon blend looks particularly elegant in a traditional setting with yew reproduction furniture trimmed with brass — the design is reminiscent of a Persian garden.

Above right. Wiltons are not necessarily plain! This neat chevron design in greens and blacks reflects the nostalgic mood for the 20's and 30's and shows just how up-to-date a traditionally woven carpet can be. The fibre blend is again 80% wool and 20% nylon and this carpet is

Cords and Carpet Tiles

As I mentioned on pages 70 and 71, there have been many developments recently in carpet construction and carpet fibres. Cord carpeting used to be made from animal hair, was mainly imported from the Continent, and, although it did not have the same luxurious pile as Wilton and Axminster, it was very hardwearing. New techniques of carpet construction and the development of synthetic fibres now means cord comes in a variety of different types. The cheapest is generally only suitable for light wear, for example bedroom use, although, if you must cover the floor cheaply, it is possible to lay it on all floors, so long as you are prepared to change it after a few years when the cord carpet begins to look shabby. It is a wise buy too if you only intend to stay in a flat or house for a few years and are unlikely to want to take the carpet with you. Also carpet buying habits are changing, and if you are the sort of person who likes to change your colour scheme fairly frequently, then it may be better to buy a fairly inexpensive cord carpet and get a new one when you redecorate (the old one may well be suitable for cutting down and fitting in another room) rather than having to plan lots of schemes round the same carpet (see page 46).

Some cords are hardwearing,

such as the type made from animal hair which has a foam backing, or the ones made from sisal; these are in the medium to expensive price range, but are not nearly as costly as an 80% wool and 20% nylon Wilton. Most cords are plain, although some of the sisals have a striped, textured or neat geometric design. They are not so luxurious under foot as Wiltons, Axminsters or most Tufteds, and sisal in particular can be rather harsh on bare feet and small bare knees, and on stairs it can be slippery, so it is not a wise choice for the hall, stairs and landing in a house where there are very young children or elderly people. Carpet tiles are a relatively new invention and are extremely practical and gaining popularity all the time. One of the advantages is that they are so versatile — you can vary your

flooring by using different colours and laying out the carpet squares in various ways. Even if you choose all one colour, if you place the tiles at right-angles to each other, the overall effect is one of a textured chequerboard.

There are two different types available — those which are loose-laid and those which are stuck to the floor. Although the loose-laid ones can sometimes kick up when furniture is moved, or catch in the vacuum cleaner, they are much more practical than those which are stuck down, since you can move them round to even out wear, you can pick them up and swill them under the tap if something is accidentally spilt on them and, if you decide to move, they can be taken up and relaid in your new home. They can be laid by a complete amateur, and are very easy to cut and fit round difficult 'obstacles' such as basins, loos etc. Loose-laid ones are less likely to kick up if you use a special 'stick-both-sides' tape, which can be stuck down crisscross fashion on the floor. Press the tile down onto the other side of the sticky tape and this will hold the carpet square in position. Incidentally all sorts of carpet construction is used for tiles; some are tufted, some are cord, others are not woven at all, but are 'compressed', some have shaggy piles, some looped or twisted, and all sorts of different fibres are used from wool to a completely new one called 'Cambrelle'.

Two ways with carpet tiles! *Left*, the corn yellow floor really is carpet-tiled, and they are all loose-laid. The chocolate-and-cream floor (*below*) shows how good a small room can look if the carpet tiles emphasize the furniture position.

Right shows some of the fascinating designs you can create on *your* floor using carpet tiles.

Carpet Care

Carpet care includes not only day-to-day cleaning, coping with spots and stains, trying to equalize wear so the carpet will not get threadbare on the piece with most 'through traffic', but

also carpet laying. It is a well-known fact that, if a carpet is not properly laid, it will not give the service it should! All carpets must have a good underlay, and the better quality this is, the more it will help to prolong the life of your carpet. It really serves the same purpose as an under-blanket on a bed, preventing any uneven surfaces of floor boards or sub-floor from causing friction

(which in turn causes wear on the pile) on the back of the carpet. There are several different types of underfelt readily available; some of the cushioned foams make a carpet feel even more luxurious underfoot, and a medium-priced carpet on a deep foam underlay can seem softer to the tread than a very expensive carpet on a cheap one. Try to buy the best quality you can afford, and remember, underfelt can be re-used so long as it is in good condition, although it must be cleaned and moved round to even out wear before the new carpet is laid. If you cannot afford underlay, then the floor can be padded with wads of newspaper and/or brown paper, but this should only be a temporary measure until an underfelt can be purchased. Never, ever, lay a new carpet on top of an old one, expecting this to do the work of an underfelt — the worn areas will quickly show through the new carpet. Special felt or foam pads are used as underlay on stairs, and newspaper should never be used in this situation.

Note: If you have underfloor central heating the underlay should be chosen with care, since some can give off an odour. In any case, in this situation, to obtain full benefit from the heating, the best treatment is a carpet 'square' or rugs combined with tiles, cork or wood.

Laying Carpets. In this era of do-it-yourself many people ask if they can lay their own carpets. Frankly, carpet laying is always better left to the professional, particularly in large or awkwardly shaped rooms. Some carpet suppliers offer a free laying service so long as carpets and underfelt are purchased from them, so it is wise to 'shop around' to get this service. Stair carpet should always be professionally laid, since this can be a danger area if a badly fitting carpet slips about. The only exception is if the stair carpet is a simple strip fitted with rods or clips, as this is easy for the amateur to lay. Remember when purchasing stair carpet, to allow about $\frac{1}{2}$ yard ($\frac{1}{2}$ m), so the carpet

can be moved up or down the stairs occasionally (about every 6 months) to even out the wear.

Some modern Latex or rubber backed carpets and cords are also easy to lay, as they don't fray when cut, so these can be laid by the amateur, so long as the room is not too large (which would mean joining the widths) nor a difficult shape — carpet tiles are very simple to lay (see previous page) so this is nearly always a do-it-yourself job.

If your home has definite 'traffic areas' — i.e. paths which all the family take to reach, say the kitchen from the living room, or across the hall from living room to kitchen, then it is worth while considering an extra carpet 'square' or rug on top of the fitted carpet to take some of the strain and prevent the carpet from becoming threadbare. Carpet 'squares' or large rugs are also practical (see page 72) as they can be turned round occasionally to alleviate wear. In a room where people watching Television tend to scuff the carpet, place a rug in front of the settee or chairs, and move furniture round occasionally.

Cleaning Carpets. During the first few weeks a new carpet tends to fluff and shed pile — don't worry as this is quite normal. Don't clean it too vigorously, nor shampoo it — give it time to settle. If a few tufts stand out above the pile, use a pair of scissors to cut them level. Never pull them out. Use a carpet sweeper for the first few weeks, then use the vacuum cleaner once or twice a week — this should be enough for the first year or two, so long as you cope with any accidents or spills immediately (see chart overleaf).

When the carpet needs cleaning, use a carpet shampoo, follow the instructions on the bottle, test first for colour-fastness, and always take care not to saturate the carpet or underlay — just use the foam from the top. Don't stand furniture back on a damp carpet as this can leave marks. If a carpet becomes very dirty, or has a stain which proves impossible to remove, have it professionally cleaned. There are many firms who specialize in this type of cleaning, and who will come to the house and deal with the problem on site. Carpet 'squares' can be taken away for professional cleaning, and some experts will remove a fitted carpet for cleaning and re-lay it again. This is only really worth while if the carpet is a very expensive one, and is also practical if you are moving and want it relaid in another house.

In a hall or on the landing there is often a 'traffic area' where the carpet tends to become worn — *left*, co-ordinated rugs have been used for maximum decorative effect, toning in each case with the colour of the fitted carpet, at the same time serving a practical purpose.

Often the area in front of the settee or chairs (used when watching television) becomes worn. *Above*, a large carpet 'square' has been laid in the sitting area, matching the plain dining area carpet, and it can be turned round occasionally to equalize wear. The toning striped rug protects the plain carpet from through 'traffic' walking from the kitchen to the sitting area.

Removing Carpet Stains

The Simple Rules

1 Have the usual stain removers handy, so that you may treat stains as soon as they occur. (Old stains will be difficult or impossible to remove).

2 Test for colourfastness before using detergents etc. (Take a few strands of each colour and put in a cup of the solution to be used, to see if the colours run.)

3 Work from the outer edges towards the centre of the stain, otherwise it may spread even further.

4 If the carpet has a rubber backing, never let any solvent reach it.

5 If you cannot remove the stain easily, don't saturate the carpet in an attempt to do so. See that the underlay is not left damp. Never replace furniture until the carpet is dry.

6 If you cannot deal with the stain satisfactorily, consult a good dry-cleaning firm as quickly as possible, telling them the cause of the stain and the treatment you have given it.

Useful stain removers

Detergents: Mix according to the manufacturer's instructions. Apply to stain on a clean cloth or sponge wrung out in the lukewarm solution, working from the outside into the centre of the stain, to prevent it spreading. Follow by using a cloth wrung out in plain water.

Carpet Shampoo: Follow carefully the manufacturer's instructions.

Dry cleaning fluid: Use sparingly, and change the cloth as it becomes soiled. Don't use near a fire or any naked flame, and work by an open window.

Grease absorbent: Sprinkle French chalk, cornflour, Fuller's earth or white talcum powder on the stain. Leave for a time, then brush out.

Borax Solution: Borax dissolves casein (the "cheese" content) which is found in milk. Sponge on a solution of 1 dessertspoon borax to $\frac{1}{2}$ pint warm water. Leave for a few minutes, sponge well with plain water, and leave to dry.

Note. If, after removing the stain, a ring appears, this is usually because the stained area is now cleaner than the rest! If you shampoo the entire carpet, the ring should then disappear.

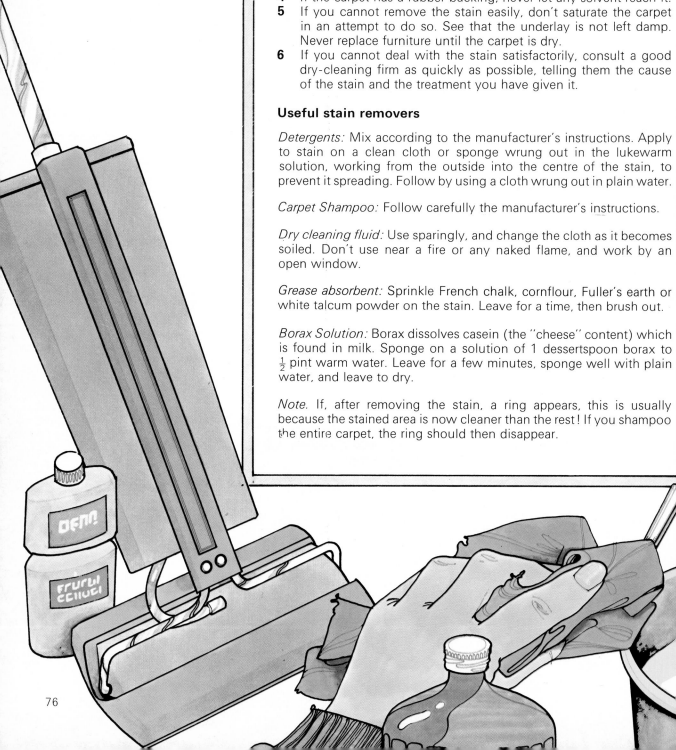

Stain	Treatment
Alcohol, including	Detergent
Beers, Wines, Spirits	Detergent
Blood	Cold water
Egg	Scrape off, then Detergent (not hot, or the stain may set)
Food (most kinds)	Detergent or carpet shampoo. Follow with grease absorbent or dry cleaning fluid if stain contains fat, milk, etc.
Grease, oil, wax	If solid, scrape off as much as possible first. Benzene.
Ink	Blot. Dust with bicarbonate of soda. Remove with brush or vacuum cleaner. Use an ink eradicator to remove final traces (test first for colour-fastness).
Metal polish	Mild detergent. Add few drops ammonia to rinsing water to neutralise acid. Leave to dry, then brush well to remove any powder.
Milk and milky drinks	Lukewarm water, if still wet, or borax if dry.
Paint	Turpentine.
Pet stains	Detergent, carpet shampoo, or special pet stain remover. Warm vinegar used afterwards often brings back the colour.
Salt solution or sea water	Detergent or carpet shampoo, with two tablespoons vinegar. (Salt may spoil the carpet dyes).
Scorch	Rub lightly with emery paper to remove damaged fibres. (Once actually destroyed by burning, they cannot be restored).
Tea, coffee, etc.	Borax, and dry cleaning fluid if liquid contained milk.
Washable ink	Methylated spirit.
Urine	Ammonia solution (one fluid ounce to one gallon warm water).
Vomit	Warm water with a few drops of ammonia added.

Firm Underfoot!

Although more homes than ever before now have fitted carpets, which reduce noise, are warm and soft underfoot, and make cleaning an easier chore (only a sweeper/vacuum cleaner is needed), there are certain areas in the home where a harder, permanent or semi-permanent floor covering is much more practical.

The permanent type includes stone, marble, terrazzo, ceramic tiles etc., and these generally last a lifetime; the semi-permanent types are wood (strip, woodblock, parquet), cork, vinyl, lino, thermoplastic, rubber etc. (many are available in tile or sheet forms), and some are more long-lasting than others! Most of the first group cannot be covered with fitted carpet, so must be chosen with care since they are likely to be a permanent fixture and many different colour and decorating schemes will have to be worked round them. Some of those in the second group (wood and cork for example) can be covered with carpet or carpet tiles when you want a change, but it is not wise to cover vinyl, lino, thermoplastic or rubber with any other form of floorcovering; far better to remove it completely, get back to the sub-floor and start again. Both thermoplastic and rubber can be difficult to remove, which should be taken into consideration when the floor covering is being chosen. Many of the above are easy for the do-it-yourself to lay, but some are not,

so if you are in doubt ask the manufacturer, and if he suggests professional help, take his advice. As flooring is such an important part of the furnishing of a house, it is worth while paying a little extra if necessary at the outset, for once it is incorrectly laid it can cost a great deal to put right.

The main advantage most of these firm floorings have over carpeting is that they can be

scrubbed, and are not affected by spills or even occasional flooding, which makes them ideal for use in halls with lots of muddy feet tramping through; bathrooms and kitchens; children's bedrooms and playrooms; utility rooms etc. Wood floors can be scrubbed if necessary, but should never be saturated with water. Rubber (seldom used in homes nowadays but often found in institutions, hall-

a natural warmth. Cork and rubber are very resilient too and tend to be less noisy than the rest of the permanent floorings, but any of them can be softened with rugs or carpet 'squares'.

The warmth of wood (*far left*) for a living room floor in a part-timbered country house, shows off the mixed furniture styles to advantage. The waxed wood-strip floor is softened by an Oriental rug.

In this kitchen/dining room (*left*) flooring is sheet vinyl, making a practical easy-to-clean surface — particularly sensible where there are young children and babies in the family.

This really luxurious bathroom with a Moroccan look has a sunken bath — the steps are painted wood to match the rest of the woodwork and walls — vinyl tiles are laid by bath and basin and softened with a washable cotton rug beside the bath.

ways of blocks of flats etc.) should not be made too wet, otherwise it will perish, and is best cleaned with a damp cloth or sponge and polished with a special emulsion polish. Cork tiles tend to swell when wet and then 'push up' so they should always be properly sealed. They can be laid in their 'natural' state and then the whole floor sealed *in situ*, or they can be purchased ready-sealed, but either type should not be made too wet once they have been laid. If you are thinking of laying a cork floor yourself, the second type is much easier for the amateur to cope with.

The majority of these floorings are fairly noisy underfoot which makes them more practical for use on the ground floor — some are heavy too (stone, terrazzo, ceramic) and consequently it is wise to use them in fairly small quantities upstairs, particularly in older houses (floor joists can always be strengthened to take them if necessary). They can also be cold to the touch, except for cork and wood which have

Plain and Patterned Floors

If you want to use pattern on the floor (see more about this in chapter 3) you can achieve really fabulous effects with the firmer floorings. Texture too, can be introduced into a scheme in this way; a woodstrip floor for example, looks quite different from a parquet floor laid herring-bone fashion, yet the two pro-

vide a warm, natural-looking texture. Cork too adds a nice rich texture to a scheme, and if you want to be adventurous you can have light and dark cork tiles, laying them chequerboard fashion or to form interesting geometric designs.

Most of the vinyls are already patterned, and need not be confined just to the bathroom or kitchen floor. They can be used on the wall as matching 'splash backs', on counter tops, on bath panels, as well as providing a practical and inexpensive floor covering for halls, children's rooms and living areas. Vinyl, lino and thermoplastic tiles give a great deal of scope for creative floor design, since they can be laid in lots of different patterns, just like carpet tiles (see page 72), and if you want a swirly, rather than a geometric pattern, sheet lino can be laid, with a pattern inset in any design you

consider to be appropriate.

Ceramic floor tiles, mosaic and terrazzo used to be very mundane floorings, but now the range is literally vast, and many of the ceramic tiles in particular are made in different, interlocking shapes (particularly the Spanish and Portuguese ones) which, even if they are all one colour, give a floor a really interesting look. Remember if you are choosing ceramic tiles with a pattern on them it is wise to see at least two or three square yards/metres laid out in the showroom, or a good coloured picture of a complete floor, before you place an order. Floor tiles are very expensive and, like patterned carpets and wallcoverings, can look very different, when laid over a large area, from a small sample of two or three tiles with which you may be tempted to make your selection.

The drawings show some of the different effects which can be achieved with wood, ceramic tiles and terrazzo tiles, and how some of them will look on the floor.

Vinyl floor tiles are easy to cut and it is possible to create the most interesting patterns with them — here a black, off-white and terracotta tile with marbled effect has been used for an unusual floor (*above left*).

Cork tiles on the floor in this luxurious room (*far left*) give texture interest and soften the rather stark ceramic-tiled walls.

Living room floors do not always have to be carpeted or tiled — sheet vinyl can be used most effectively, so long as the design is carefully chosen to enhance the furniture and furnishings. Generally the type of pattern which resembles traditional ceramic tiles is the most successful in this situation.

SURE & SIMPLE HOMEMAKING

Room to Breathe!

Space is at such a premium these days, and many families find they need more room as the children begin to grow up and want somewhere to play or pursue hobbies; a quiet area is often needed for reading or doing homework, while other members of the family want to watch television or listen to music. Most boys and girls would prefer their own bedroom and I am sure there isn't a parent who would not be delighted to have a separate playroom for their children! And what may have seemed an adequate kitchen for a young married couple simply won't stretch to take those extras; washing machines, dishwashers, deep-freezes, which suddenly seem essential equipment when you have a healthy, growing family.

Of course one answer is to move to a bigger house, but this can be costly. Finding the right house in the same area is sometimes impossible and it may not be practical to move further afield, so what is the answer? To extend your existing house may well be the solution, and there are various ways of doing this. Probably one of the easiest is to put a simple prefabricated one-storey extension on the back of the property, which can be used to extend the living room, or as a separate dining room, study, garden room or conservatory; or you might prefer to enlarge the kitchen, making a dining or 'utility' area in the extra space. If funds allow, you could extend right across the back of the house, adding extra space onto the kitchen *and* the living area. This would be more complicated than the do-it-yourself type of extension and would probably involve the services of an architect or surveyor to draw up plans, and a professional builder to carry them out. Proper plans would be essential, since these have to be passed by the local council before the work can be started — in fact planning permission has to be granted for almost every type of extension, so the first step is to consult your local authority before starting even the smallest additions (for more about extensions see page 88).

If there is no room to build out the back, then it might be possible to extend upwards and open up the loft, or build over an integral garage, with access from the existing staircase. Again planning permission will have to be sought and it is wise to call in the experts for professional help right at the outset — there are specialist firms who do nothing except loft conversions for example.

If the roof is pitched too low, or you don't have a garage, it may still be possible to convert and extend. Sometimes an extension on the side of the house can combine a new staircase, a downstairs utility room or cloakroom and a bathroom upstairs, with the old hall becoming an integral part of one of the downstairs rooms and giving extra storage space and a second bathroom upstairs.

Remember, when you build onto an existing room, the colour scheme in the extension must tone, even if there are doors between the two rooms. In this picture (*left*), a prefabricated extension has been added, making the living room much larger. This is now used only for sitting and the extension has become a dining area. The majority of the walls are white, including the original wall of the house and carpet tiles in a bold geometric design continue from the sitting into the dining area, but the part of the floor under the dining table has a practical sheet vinyl which tones perfectly with the carpet tiles.

Right, the deliciously fresh conservatory extension was added onto the side of the house and the hall wall opened up to give a verdant vista. Meals are taken in the conservatory in

the summer, so it is furnished with white wrought-iron garden furniture which links with the hall table and umbrella stand. Note the rattan blinds to screen the conservatory from too much sun — a wise precaution with any extension which has a lot of glass.

An Illusion of Space

It is possible to make even the smallest house, bungalow or flat appear more spacious simply by the way you decorate and choose your schemes. Co-ordinated colours are the secret and, if your home is very small, use fresh, pale colours and start with the floor-covering — lay the same colour throughout, or certainly throughout the ground floor, up the stairs and on to the landing. In a slightly larger house, if you want to mix pattern and plain on the floors, then make sure you co-ordinate your choice of carpets properly. A patterned carpet in the hall and on the stairs and landing could carry through into the dining room, with a plain but *toning* carpet in the sitting room; bedroom carpets could then be in different plain colours to pick out the various shades in the

stair/landing carpet. If you do not want to renew your floor coverings, then try to carry colours through from room-to-room on the walls, in furniture or furnishings and accessories. Remember the hall is the part of the home which creates the first impact, so if it appears small and cluttered, then this will be the impression given of the whole house. Aim for a warm, welcoming but spacious atmosphere in this area of the home — even if it means cheating with mirrors or knocking down part of a wall (see pages 12 and 13). Try to carry this impression through into the living room and

Lower left: Wallpaper and fabrics that go together can be used to help create an illusion of space. In this terrace house, part of the wall between the dining room and hall has been removed. The colour scheme is based on cool greens, with a plain carpet laid throughout. The wallpaper on the dining room wall is echoed in the tablecloth, while the hall curtains are in a specially designed companion fabric.

Below: In this hall, soft browns and greens have been used with white for maximum effect. The main walls have been painted with a matt emulsion in a soft coffee-brown with the archway picked out in a pale apple-green, and the staircarpet, with its muted pattern, links with the wall colours. The pale tile-effect floor covering in the hall is, in fact, a sheet vinyl, so it is practical to clean as well as adding to the atmosphere of space and light. The simple curtains echo the colours of wall and flooring.

then nobody will notice how small the other rooms are!

Top right: Co-ordinated carpets help give continuity of colour throughout the house, creating a feeling of spaciousness. The patterned Axminster carpet is in subtle shades of green, from soft leaf to dark moss, the palest colour has been used for the walls in the dining room. The plain Wilton sitting room carpet is in a subtle shade of soft olive, which tones perfectly with the patterned carpet.

Upper left: In this older-style house, the floors are woodblock, so the colour schemes have been linked to the Oriental rugs in shades of reds, blues, gold and white. The sitting room (which is partially open-plan with the hall) and the dining room are painted in a rich pinky-red with lots of brilliant white paintwork. The upholstery, in shades of gold and red, and the blue hall walls, echo these colours in the rugs.

Can I 'Open up' my Living Room with Glass?

Another way of making downstairs rooms appear more spacious is to install really large sliding glass 'patio' doors or a picture window; even the smallest room is improved by this treatment. If you build an attractive terrace immediately outside the living room, then you can make this patio an integral part of the room, even in the winter. In the summer meals can be enjoyed *al fresco* and the area becomes an outdoor dining room with easy access from the living area. However, large areas of glass can be very cold in winter as the heat in the room is automatically drawn outside. In summer, the hot sun beating down through a picture window can make a room unbearably hot and stuffy, and can cause fading of furniture and carpets if these are not absolutely colourfast. Consequently there must be some form of 'screen' between the glass and the room, as well as curtains to cover the whole area on cold winter nights. Proper double-glazing is expensive but, with this type of window or door, worth every penny. The 'sandwich' type is the most effective, where air is trapped between two layers of glass and the whole permanently bonded together into one well-fitting unit. Metal frames are best for this type, since they can expand and contract depending on weather conditions. Apart from the extra insulation provided, it is an excellent idea to have blinds next to the glass, under full-length curtains which can be lined with special insulated lining or even inter-lined to keep the cold out and the warmth in! The type of blind you choose depends on personal likes and dislikes and the style of the room scheme and furnishings but, as a general rule, roller blinds are not practical in very wide widths, which leaves venetian blinds as the most sensible choice. These now come with vertical as well as horizontal slats which can be drawn back or even parted in the centre, like curtains, and can be angled at the pull of a cord, to diffuse or reflect light as required.

Below: Vertical venetian blinds are used to screen an entire 'wall of glass' in this living room, but they draw back just like curtains for easy access to the garden. Maximum width is 15 ft (4·6 m) and maximum drop 20 ft (6·1 m). If your window is larger than this, buy a pair so they divide in the centre!

Bring the garden indoors! In this living room (*right*) sliding glass doors lead on to the terrace. The floor has carpet tiles, laid chequerboard fashion to link visually with the patio floor, cool garden greens have been used for the colour scheme and lots of plants add a further verdant touch; furniture is elegant conservatory style.

When this 1930's house was modernised, the fireplace, on an outside wall, was faced with brick, the ceiling clad with wood, and the two recesses on each side of the chimney breast (which originally had 'port hole' windows) were fitted with non-openable glass panels down to the floor, with arched windows above, so the garden can be enjoyed from the sitting area. There are sliding french-doors to a terrace at the opposite end of the room (*below right*).

Extending Outwards... and Upwards!

Extending outwards, so long as you have adequate space, is usually easier than extending upwards. There are basically two sorts of extension; one is the prefabricated type, often in timber, which comes ready for home assembly, and the other is a proper extra room in brick to match the original structure. The former can be put up by a competent do-it-yourselfer and his or her 'mate', although some building firms undertake this work. The fact that an extension is 'prefabricated' does not mean it has to be a certain shape or size, some of the firms manufacturing extensions will prepare special designs to order, but based on the 'knock-down' principle. A brick-built extension is normally a job for the professional builder, but is not necessarily beyond the scope of the amateur who has a knowledge of bricklaying; the secret is to use ready-made joinery (window frames, door frames etc.) and a simple roofing system.

Whichever type you choose, planning permission is generally necessary, and the Building Regulations are fairly stringent concerning such things as fire risk, so the first step is to consult the local council, and ask them for the necessary forms for planning permission plus any explanatory leaflets. If your extension is prefabricated, then the firm supplying it will submit suitable plans; for a brickbuilt one you will have to get plans drawn up, and remember you will need a set of original house plans of the property, so you can show the council exactly where the extension is being added. Many councils insist on 'before' and 'after' type plans. If you don't have a set of plans of your property, you can always obtain these, either from the builder who originally built the house (if he is still in business) or from the local council, who would have a set on file, so long as the house is not too old!

One very important thing to remember when you are building an extension on to existing rooms is that it will take a lot of light away from those rooms — in fact an already dark one could look like the 'Black Hole of Calcutta', so keep the extension as light as possible. This means lots of glass, so it is often worthwhile investing in double-glazing as well as good blinds (see pages 86/87), and consequently this room will need adequate heating — often an existing central heating system will be efficient enough to allow for extra radiators in the extension, but the type which have a built-in convector fan are even more practical as they blow out hot air (these are run off the existing heating system). Alternatives are night storage heaters or electric convectors with an electric oil-filled radiator to keep the chill off. Remember to plan a colour scheme which will tone with the rooms leading into the extension (see page 82/83), and as most extensions lead out directly into the garden, always choose a practical floorcovering.

Building a room in the roof is not really a do-it-yourself job, but there are firms who specialize in this type of work and who will come to your home and give advice, submit plans and a free estimate. If you accept it, they will negotiate with the local council (planning permission and Building Regulations apply just as much to extending upwards as outwards) and carry out the work. Builders will also undertake loft conversions and

they will probably be able to draw plans for you, or you can get a surveyor or architect to do this. The pitch of the roof is all-important when it comes to this type of conversion; with some roofs it simply is not possible to get enough head-room, so they cannot be converted. The other important thing is finding space for the stairs to go up into the loft — you may well lose space from another room below, so the extension would only be worth while if you have a large enough loft to compensate for this loss (some attics can be divided into 2 or more rooms). A spiral staircase is sometimes a practical answer, but this has to conform to the local Building Regulations and needs quite a large square area for the treads to rise, allowing head room for passage underneath. This type of staircase has to rise onto a landing which often means the loft cannot be closed off from the rest of the house, so all the warmth could float upwards! This is another important consideration with loft conversions, the walls and ceilings must be well insulated, which is one good reason for cladding them with wood and roof insulating material can be packed down between the wood (because it is fixed by battens) and the outside wall.

Note: converting a loft means the rest of the house may well be in chaos for a time, as materials have to be taken up through the house. If you can't face this, they can be taken up outside, but this means scaffoldings, winches etc., which greatly adds to the cost.

Top Left: An extension built onto an existing property. Lots of windows, all double-glazed and fitted with blinds, give good light in rooms leading into the extension. The exterior house wall has been faced with wood cladding and the floor is practical sealed cork tiles, softened with rugs.

Above: A really superb bedroom made in the roof; the special 'roof windows' allow good ventilation and light without the necessity of building a dormer. Note the interesting curtain treatment, where a second curtain pole keeps the drapes from falling forward, still allowing the elegant treatment of full-length curtains.

Left: Living room in a loft is part of a house conversion; the attic in a Victorian house was large enough to make into a self-contained flat and the interior has been given a modern look with horizontal wood cladding giving extra insulation.

Light and Bright!

The importance of successful lighting is often underestimated. A colour scheme may look marvellous in daylight, but if the room is poorly lit at night it can suddenly appear drab and dull. Good lighting, on the other hand, contributes enormously to a room, it sets the mood, is the magic touch which brings the colours and textures of your furnishings to life, and is something which can be used generously since running costs are not high despite increased electricity charges. On the purely practical, rather than the aesthetic side, adequate lighting makes a home a safer place in which to live!

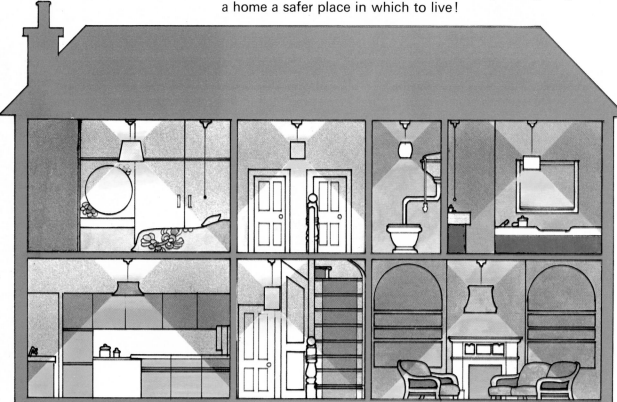

As lighting should be an integral part of the decorative scheme, and not just something plugged in afterwards, the best time to plan your lighting is when you are building a house, or converting or decorating a room. As mentioned in Chapter 1, this is also the time to decide on the position of the various items of furniture, and once you have a squared plan of the room (or rooms) with furniture positioned on it, you can decide exactly what sort of lighting to have, and where you want it. You can, of course, improve a lighting scheme at any time, but then there may be problems about concealing cable; trailing flexes and over-loaded plugs are dangerous and should be avoided at all costs.

Your aim should be to provide as flexible a system as possible, particularly in areas like the living room and bedroom, so that different lamps and lights can be turned on and off at different times, creating various

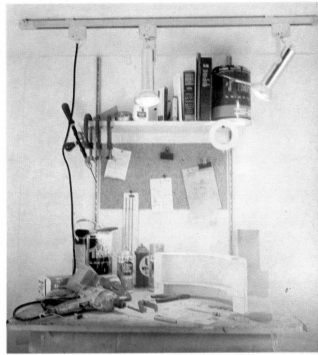

atmospheres. For example, a living room can be light and bright whilst the family are talking, knitting, sewing, or younger children playing; but at the flick of a switch or two it should be possible to create an intimate atmosphere with soft background illumination, suitable for relaxing and listening to music or watching television.

Other areas of the home need good clear lighting, the kitchen and bathroom for example, and food cannot be prepared nor the washing up done efficiently without adequate light. In the hall it is essential to have good lighting to avoid accidents on the stairs, but this does not mean a relentlessly glaring light which shows up every defect! On the next few pages you will find lighting ideas room-by-room, but don't forget to include lighting in your overall plan. Good lighting for the patio or terrace means you can make the most of the garden in the evening and, on the practical side, the front door should be well lit so that the name of the home, or number, shows up clearly at night. The garage and any out-

houses need adequate lighting.

Top: Light exactly where you need it can be provided by spotlights on a track, so they can be adjusted if necessary. This is an ideal treatment for a kitchen worksurface and a workbench, as well as providing light for a desk, drawing board or

mirror.

Above: In this living room, recessed ceiling lights provide pleasant background lighting, the lamp can be lowered over the dining table when necessary, and all other lighting comes from strategically placed table lamps and spotlights.

How do I Plan Light for Living?

The main point to remember when planning lighting for living areas is the need for different types of light fittings. A central ceiling light on its own provides somewhat poor lighting for activities around the edges of the room. There should be some form of background lighting (some of which can be switched from the door of the room) and this can be provided by wall lights. These are complicated and therefore rather expensive to install as the wires have to be buried in a channel cut in the wall and plastered over, a proceeding best carried out with extensive re-decoration or when making structural alterations. Other background lighting can be provided by illuminating alcoves or recesses with small concealed strip lights (china cabinets, shelves and units can all be similarly lit); or spotlights can be used for this purpose and to draw attention to a special painting, picture or wallhanging. Curtains can be dramatised with a pelmet fitting.

See above: An intimate atmosphere is created by strategically placed lamps in this modern sitting area.

Background lighting alone is not enough for most living areas. There must be good light for sewing or reading for example, and this can be provided by fairly large table lamps. These need to fit in with the furnishing and decorative scheme, but the lampshade must allow maximum light to pass through it. A glass shade with an opalescent or pierced effect can look very pretty and allows a soft clear light to fall exactly where it is needed, and a simple drum shade in a fairly pale colour with a white interior reflects light effectively. Standard lamps, preferably adjustable in height are also practical, since they are easily portable and can be moved round when required; placed behind a chair or settee they give really good directional light. However, to enable these portable lamps, both table and standard, to be moved around without trailing long lengths of flex across the floor, you must have enough socket outlets.

The dining table must not be forgotten; here the best lighting is a lamp on a rise-and-fall fitting which can be pulled down, over the table at meal times. This gives a sparkle to glass and china and creates a pleasantly intimate atmosphere for entertaining, but make sure that the light is not shining directly into the diners' eyes. The sideboard or serving table should also be adequately lit; a good table lamp, spotlights or wall lights each side of the serving hatch (if you have one) could be the best solution.

The hall, stairs and landing is another important area; usually the hall light does double duty, illuminating the stairs as well, so it should have a two-way switch from the front door and the landing. Here again there should be some background lighting, with a really good but not glaring light, to illuminate the stairs. If you have a telephone in the hall, you will need some form of light to switch on when taking messages; consider a desk lamp on table or shelf, or a wall or spotlight. Another black spot in most homes is the familiar cupboard-under-the-stairs; have an automatic light fitted to the door jamb which comes on as soon as the door is opened.

Lighting for Bedroom, Bathroom

The most important consideration when thinking about the bedroom is to have soft background lighting which can be controlled from both door and bed; really good light at the dressing table or basin; and lamps for reading in bed. If it is a double bed there should be one on each side, individually controlled.

For background lighting, rather than the dreary and now old-fashioned centre light, consider pelmet lighting (set about 12 inches (30 cm) in front of the fabric) which will illuminate the curtains at night, giving a soft glow round the window area. If you are going to have curtains suspended on poles, this is not practical, but you can have spotlights at ceiling height, trained to shine on the curtains, or they can be suspended on track each side of the window, making them adjustable. Whichever you choose, it should be double-switched at the door and bed.

The ideal lighting for the dressing table is one which illuminates the whole face seen in the mirror, leaving no part of it in deep shadow. One fitting is never enough and the best arrangement for making up the face is the theatrical mirror which has a frame of tungsten bulbs set all round. This treatment is scarcely practical, nor pretty enough for most bedrooms, although if you decorate in 30's 'green-room' style you could include a theatrical mirror. Almost the same effect can be achieved by having fluorescent lighting on three sides of the dressing table mirror, or spotlights set on either side which can be adjusted to focus directly on the face.

Bedside lamps must be stable, and switch on easily when one has to fumble in the dark. It may be more practical to have wall lights above the bed, placed so there is enough clearance for sitting up in bed. Fluorescent tubes in diffusers run just above head height along the top of the bed is another alternative. Spotlights can also be used as bedside lamps, individually adjusted, and again, spotlight mounted on track is worth considering.

The other type of light well worth having in the bedroom is one inside the wardrobe or built-in cupboards, enabling you to see the contents clearly during the daytime as well as at night! This type of light can be worked by a switch in the door jamb, so it automatically comes on when the door is opened.

In the Bathroom safety is of primary importance; the fittings must be absolutely safe so there is no danger of electric shock through touching conductive materials with wet hands. All the electrical equipment in the bathroom should have a pull-cord switch or one which is controlled outside the room. The main fitting, which is switched from the door or outside, should be centrally placed and ideally set flush with, or recessed into, the ceiling.

The mirror over the basin or vanitory unit needs to be similar to the one described for the dressing table, providing a good light for shaving and making up. In the bathroom it is possible to set the mirror on deep battens, and the fluorescent tube can be run just behind the edges; this gives all round light and the warmth of the tube helps to

nd Kitchen

keep the mirror free from condensation. Alternatively a fluorescent strip can be concealed behind a pelmet which runs along the top of the mirror and can be continued along the wall and across the top of the window if desired.

In the Kitchen most of the work, preparing food, washing up, cooking etc., takes place against the walls, so all too often you will find you are working in your own light if the only light is from a central ceiling fitting, however good. A fluorescent tube at ceiling height, which is controlled from the door to the room and the back door (if there is access outside from the kitchen) makes an excellent background light, but try to have another light over the cooker and one over the sink. These could well be spotlights, or, if the kitchen is large, consider three smaller fluorescent lights; circular as well as tubular fittings are available. Also try to light work surfaces individually. Where there are wall cupboards mounted over a counter top, conceal strip lights (controlled separately) *under* the top cupboards. Again spotlights can be used to light worktops which do not have wall units over them.

If the kitchen includes a dining area or breakfast bar, then the ideal arrangement is a lamp on a rise-and-fall fitting which can be pulled down over the centre of the table at meal times.

Some General Points to Consider

When buying lamps choose only those marked with the electricity voltage of your locality.

A 100-watt lamp is the correct size for table lamps and pendant ceiling fittings in smaller rooms. Standard lamps usually take 150-watt bulbs. 40 or 60 watt is the best size for wall-bracket fittings, but if the shades are small and the other lighting in the room is good 25-watt bulbs may be sufficient.

Clear lamps are not suitable for domestic use except where you want to create hard shadows and a bright sparkle — with a chandelier fitting, for example. Pearl lamps are the best buy as they give a softer, but not lesser amount of light than clear lamps.

Internally silica-coated lamps give soft, diffused light. For a flattering warm light, buy a pink-tinted type. Coiled-coil filament lamps are a little more expensive than single-coil lamps but they give up to 20% more light for the same amount of current.

Reflector spotlight lamps can be let into the ceilings for spotlight use. They are available in 75 and 100-watt size. For use on either side of mirrors, use single cap tubular lamps in 40 or 60 wattages. Double-cap tubular lamps are suitable for use in alcoves or china cupboards where they are unseen. They are available in clear or frosted finish in 30 or 60-watt sizes.

Candle lamps are for use with candelabra-type ceiling or wall fittings. So long as they are used well above eye-level they can be used without shades. They can be bought in either a clear or frosted finish, in plain or 'twisted' shapes in 25, 40 or 60-watt sizes.

Architectural tubular lamps are intended for use with mirrors, shelf units, curtain pelmets. No shades are needed for them.

Fluorescent lamps have an internal fluorescent coating and it is this that regulates the amount and colour of the light.

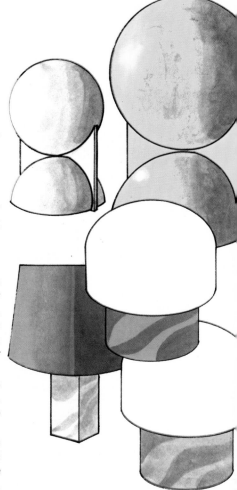

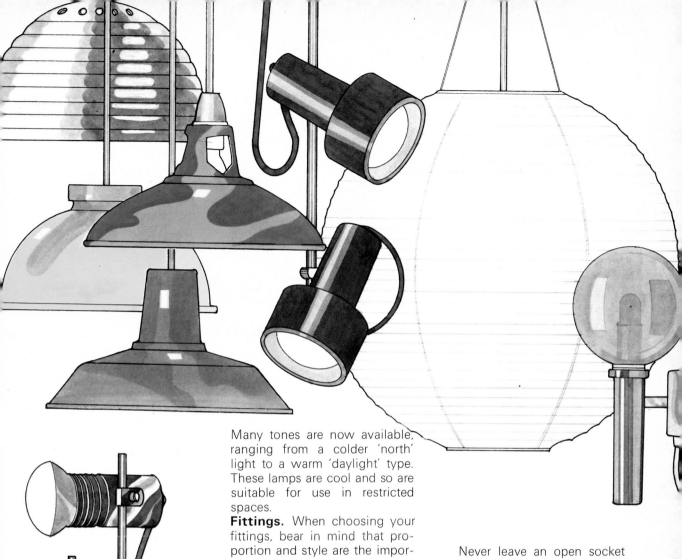

Many tones are now available, ranging from a colder 'north' light to a warm 'daylight' type. These lamps are cool and so are suitable for use in restricted spaces.

Fittings. When choosing your fittings, bear in mind that proportion and style are the important factors. Simple shades and lamp bases will combine happily with all types of interior decoration. If standard or table lamps, they should stand firmly. Shades should give as much light as possible without glare, and for standard and table lamps they should have a wide opening at top and bottom. Whatever colour the exterior, a white lining is best, to give the maximum amount of reflected light. In general, fabric shades are chosen for the softer, diffused light they give, which makes them more suitable for background use than direct lighting. All shades should be easily detachable for cleaning.

Safety Precautions. Never allow wiring to become frayed. When it does show signs of wear, replace it entirely — don't rely on temporary patches with insulating tape.

Never leave an open socket 'live' where there are children about.

Never try to mend a fuse before switching off at the main, and always keep torch, fuse wire and a small insulated screwdriver to hand near the fusebox.

Modern Developments

There have been many developments with lighting in the last few years, in particular the invention of track which is intended to take spotlights, but which also allows other items to be plugged into the circuit as well (see pages 90/91). Furniture has also been produced which has built-in lighting, so unit furniture for example, can have soft diffused lighting to illuminate a special collection, or to provide background lighting. The units (*above left*) are a good example.

97

Window Dressing

Curtains are as important to a room as clothes are to a woman, and yet it is surprising how often they are the most neglected feature in a home! Apart from their practical purpose of controlling light, shutting out a cold damp atmosphere, making a room more intimate and cosy and ensuring privacy, curtains can, with a little thought and planning, beautify an unattractive window, camouflage a dismal view, help alter the proportions of a badly-shaped room, and provide a face lift for a tired scheme.

Nothing looks worse than limp, skimpy curtains hanging dejectedly from a naked track, so take a good look at your windows and decide on curtain styling before you think about buying the fabric. All curtains should be as full as possible — at least $1\frac{1}{2}$ times the width of the curtain *track* (not the window), but better still, twice the width. The most elegant curtains are floor-length ones, and although it is not always practical to have full-length lined kitchen and bathroom curtains, those in the main living rooms and bedrooms should always be lined; for extra luxury and insulation they can be interlined or lined with a special insulated lining fabric. The exception is the sheer, textured and open weave fabric which is intended to let the light filter through, and so is not lined; these curtains look best combined with blinds, to give privacy at night.

Length

Floor-length curtains always look best, and these should finish $\frac{1}{2}$ inch (13 mm) to 1 inch (25 mm) from the carpet or floor. It may not be practical to have full-length curtains, so if they are to be short they should just touch the sill as curtains hanging a few inches below the sill look tatty. Remember to make large enough hems to allow for shrinkage in cleaning; also heavy hems make the curtains hang better and special weights can be sewn into the hems for a really professional look. When measuring to determine the length of the finished curtain, measure from the *track* to the sill or floor and not just from the top of the window.

Window Width

Unless the window stretches from wall to wall you will need a curtain track or pole which extends beyond each side of the window to enable the curtains to be pulled well back during the daytime, this is particularly important in rooms which lack light. There is no set rule about the additional length of track required, since this will depend on the bulk of the fabric used and whether you want the curtains to pull completely clear of the window frame or not. However a good guide is to allow at least 6 inches (150 mm) of extra track on *each* side of a very small, narrow window, at least 12 inches (300 mm) on *each* side of a medium-sized window and at least 18 inches (450 mm) on *each* side of a wide window. With bay windows it is often practical to place the track at ceiling height and 'cut-off' the bay with the curtains at night, thereby cutting heat loss.

Curtain Width and Fullness

Curtains should always be generously full so, if you are working on a tight budget, it may be better to buy plenty of an inexpensive fabric rather than not enough of an expensive one! The total width of the finished curtains is determined by (and must always be calculated from) the width of the track and *not* from the window width. The type of curtain heading chosen

also affects the amount of fabric you will need in each curtain. *Gathered Headings* need a minimum of 1½ times the width of the track, divided between the two curtains, but twice the width gives a more pleasing result. *Pencil-pleated Headings* require 2½ times the width of the track divided between the two curtains, and *Pinch-pleated Headings* require at least double the track width, but often more, depending on the type of pleating used.

Note. These comments still apply if you plan to buy ready-made curtains!

Curtains in a modern living room (*left*) hang from ceiling-to-floor although the window is not full-length. The fabric matches the wallpaper and the curtains have been made so the design continues along the window wall, making a most attractive and cosy dining area.

Elegant self-striped fabric is made up into floor-length curtains with pinch-pleated headings (*top left*). When they are closed at night, the effect is of a complete wall of richly draped fabric, and it is doubly effective because it is reflected in the full-length mirror.

Sill-length curtains (*top right*) are used at a bay in this older-style house, so maximum benefit can be enjoyed from the radiator underneath (hidden by the cane settee). Leaded-light windows, such as these look best with simple country-style curtain treatments.

High, narrow ranch-style windows (*above*) can be hard to 'dress'. Here the treatment is very simple — neatly gathered curtains on white plastic track — eye-catching pictures detract from the fact the window is 'blind'.

Which Style for My Window?

Most homes don't have 'problem windows' as such, but it can be very difficult to decide on the right style of curtain for the basic window types. Obviously the fabric will be chosen to complement the colour scheme and the style of furnishing, so the curtains must be designed as an integral part of the decor. In a Victorian house with large sash windows, elegant velvet curtains hung on poles would look right, but a casement window with lattice panes in a country cottage needs short, flounced curtains, possibly in a pretty chintz or gingham check.

One of the best ways of deciding on curtain styling is to take a long critical look at your window, then sketch it out on a piece of paper, and try various curtain styles until you get the right effect for both the window and your room scheme.

A Bay or Bow Window is often difficult to 'dress' satisfactorily (see Page 99). In the two pictures showing an angular bay the curtain treatment is quite different yet equally attractive. *Lower left,* the curtains are short-to-the-sill, suspended under a simple pelmet; crisp nets conceal a view from the street. A window-seat makes

the most of what could be wasted space. In the *upper left* drawing, curtains with pencil-pleated headings are suspended from a pole which has track concealed inside it. The curtains close off the bay at night. Again crisp nets provide a screen, and these are sill-length even though the curtains are full-length.

On the bow-fronted window, *above top,* curtains with pinch-pleated headings are suspended by rings from an old-fashioned wooden pole, and pretty short frilled nets soften the window without completely screening it. This would be an ideal treatment for a bedroom window in an

older-style house.

Casement Windows can be treated in several ways. Here we show a modern and a traditional way of window dressing! *Centre left*, the full-length pencil-pleated curtains, trimmed with braid, pull back to clear the window during the daytime. The track is the modern 'invisible' type which seems to 'melt' into the window frame. In the cottage *above top*, the curtains are short and flounced with a pretty frilled valance to match.

Sash Windows are another difficult type to 'dress' satis-

factorily. The simplest way *above* is a sill-length curtain with pencil-pleated heading, which can be suspended from the 'invisible' type of track. This looks effective in a hall, a bedroom, or where a very simple uncluttered effect is needed. For a dramatic touch, *top right*, floor-to-ceiling curtains under a scalloped pelmet look very elegant. If the radiator is immediately under a window, a roller blind to match (or contrast with) the curtains, can be a practical extra. On cold winter nights the curtains can be drawn to the edge of the radiator, and the blind pulled down to the

sill, so the heat is not merely warming the curtains! When a sash window looks out onto a drab wall or unsightly view, café curtains can be the answer. The short curtain is mounted on pole or track on the bar of the sash and is kept permanently drawn across the window. In this drawing *lower right* the sill-length curtains are suspended from a pole and have self-coloured backs. When they are closed at night the double layer of fabric acts as extra insulation. *Note.* Café curtains can, of course, be used on most types of window and need not be confined to sash windows only.

Top Treatments!

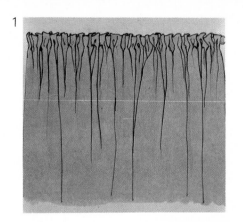

The heading at the top of the curtain is an integral part of the styling, and there are many different ways of treating it. If you plan to have a pelmet, whether this be in fabric, wood, hardboard etc.; or a frilled or pleated valance to match the curtains; or draped 'swags and tails'; the actual curtain heading will be concealed, and so it would be a waste to use anything but the ordinary standard heading tape which gathers up the fabric in soft folds (*Fig. 1*). On the other hand, if you plan to use a neat curtain track of the 'invisible' type (see page 101) then the heading should

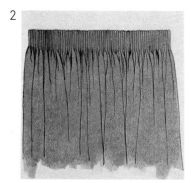

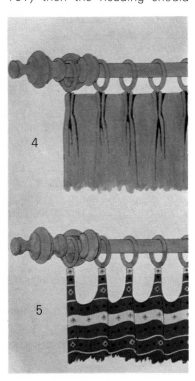

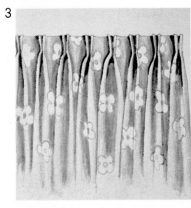

be pleated and preferably designed to stand up slightly above the track, to hide it when the curtains are closed. There are several different types of pleating you can use, the most popular being pencil pleats, which look very crisp and are best used on a light-weight fabric since they reduce the width considerably by gathering up the curtain tightly (thick fabric would be too bulky); and pinch pleats, which can be double, triple or even quadruple! These look like pretty fan pleating at the top of the curtain (*Figs. 2 and 3*).

Either type of heading can be done by hand, but there are many easy-to-use heading tapes now available which do the job for you. Some have to be pleated up by using pronged hooks, but others are specially woven so when the draw strings in the tape are pulled up and knotted the heading automatically pleats up, and ordinary hooks can be used to hang the curtains. Full instructions for using either type of tape are given by the manufacturers, either in the form of a special leaflet or printed on the box containing the tape and hooks. If you are using a curtain pole, then again the heading ought to be a decorative one, although it should not obscure the pole since this is intended to be part of the overall effect of the drapes. There are many different types of pole, in wood, metal, plastic; some have rings, with a little hole in them into which curtain hooks can be slipped, others have rings which have to be sewn to the curtain, and another type has a concealed track inside it which takes ordinary hooks. Headings can be pleated, as previously described, or scalloped (*Figs. 4, 5*).

A very narrow window in a dining room *centre left* has plain red curtains to match the walls, with a pelmet board in the same colour to make the window look less tall and narrow.

Two ways with poles and garden doors! A single curtain with pinch-pleated heading is suspended by rings from a white painted pole, *bottom left*. Sliding patio doors also have a single curtain, *below*, with pencil-pleated heading suspended from a pole with concealed track inside.

French doors often have little side windows as well, *above* and it may be hard to know how to dress these windows. Plan for a complete wall of fabric when the curtains are closed and make floor-to-ceiling curtains with pleated headings suspended from a brass pole which clears the top of all the windows.

Choosing Fabrics, Measuring and Making Up

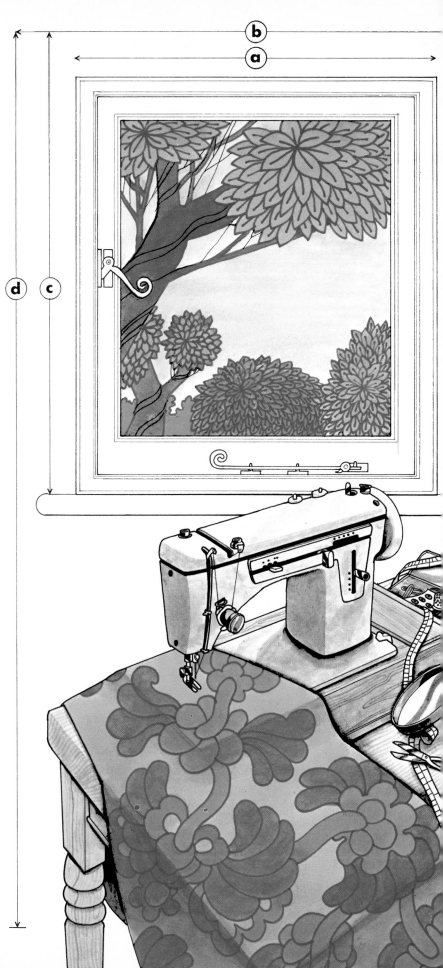

Having decided on curtain style and top treatments, then comes the fun of choosing the right fabric. Colour and design are naturally a matter of personal taste; for guidance on colour, pattern and plain see Chapters 2 and 3, but try to choose a curtain fabric which you will enjoy living with, which will enhance the present decoration scheme and tone with future ones.

Always choose fabric (and lining) which has been specifically made for curtains since it will wear well, should be colourfast, and drape and hang well. Dress fabrics may be very pretty and often less expensive than furnishing fabrics, but they do not have the necessary 'body' and can fade and rot if exposed to strong sunlight and/or condensation.

In the shop, hold a length of fabric up to assess drapability, and enquire about the methods of cleaning and whether the fabric is pre-shrunk and colourfast. If you are in doubt take home a sample, not only for colour-matching, but to test washability. In some shops you may have to buy a small piece for testing, but it is worth while spending a little at this stage to make sure the fabric is exactly right.

Pattern Matching

Remember if you choose a fabric with a definite pattern this has to be matched not only when you are joining widths of fabric together, but also from curtain to curtain and from window to window if there are several in the same room. This often means buying quite a lot of extra fabric to allow for matching, and the off-cuts can be used up for cushions, lampshades etc. If you are working to a tight budget it may be wise to choose a plain or vertical striped fabric, or one with a fairly small pattern repeat! Join widths when necessary, using an open or french seam.

Fabric	Machine Needle
Heavy	Singer size 16, Continental size 100
Medium to light	Singer size 14, Continental size 90
Light	Singer size 14 or 11, Continental size 90 or 80.

Measuring Up

All curtain measurements start with the track (see page 98), so first of all you need to get this measurement correct. Length will depend on whether you are having sill or floor-length curtains, but if possible use a yard-stick or metal rule rather than a tape measure and get another member of the family to write down and check your measurements. Measure the window following the diagram, jot these down on a piece of paper and take them with you when you shop. Most fabric salesmen are highly competent at calculating the correct amount of fabric, but you will obviously want some idea of the amount you will need and the salesman can double-check for you. Fullness will depend on the type of heading you are having, but it is better to work on maximum fullness so allow at least twice the length of the *track* (measurement b) for plain gathered headings, and at least $2\frac{1}{2}$ times the width for pleated headings. This will give you the number of widths of fabric you require. To calculate length you will need to add on extra to measurement c or d to allow for the hem and heading — say 6 in (15 cm) for hem, plus 2–4 in. (5–10 cm) for the heading; more — 6 in. (15 cm) for a deep-pleat heading. To work out the total, take the number of widths and multiply by the total length, remembering to allow for pattern matching.

Making up Curtains

A sewing machine is essential for curtain making and it is necessary to use the correct size needle for the type of curtain fabric or the stitching will pucker. See table below.

Other equipment required is large cutting out scissors, pins, a tape measure, needles, a thimble, matching thread to curtain fabric.

In most homes the cutting out has to be done on the floor for adequate space. Lay the fabric out full width and measure one length (remembering to allow for headings and hems). Pull a thread across top and bottom to ensure that the curtain will hang straight. Match all the other lengths (adjusting for pattern continuation if necessary) along the first length you measured. Pull a thread or loose tack across the width before cutting the lengths.

Curtains should be made up in the following order:

1. First snip selvedge and seam the widths of the curtains together. If half widths are used, ensure that they will lie on the outer edges of the window frame.

2. Attach headings according to instructions which will vary according to whether you want the headings to cover or reveal the curtain track. The heading tape should be tacked or pinned before sewing. When you are sure that it is straight, leaving an even amount of curtain at the top, turn the "centre of window" end of the tape under and stitch it firmly to the curtain. Knot the cords loosely at the other end. The cords at the outer ends of the curtain must be left uncut to pull the curtain heading together. When the curtain is finally pleated, do not cut the cords. Knot them loosely and tuck them neatly behind the curtain. The cords can then be unloosened and the curtain pulled flat for washing and cleaning.

3. Turn in the side hems stopping about 10 ins (25 cm) above the bottom of the curtain to allow for the turn up of the bottom hems. Press the seams and the side hems flat.

4. Turn up bottom hem and pin, but do not sew. Put in hooks, hang curtains and allow hems to 'drop' for a few days, adjust if necessary and hem by hand. To line curtains see next page.

Lining Curtains

Lining preserves the life of a curtain, prevents it from fading, increases insulation and makes it hang much better; it also has the advantage of making all the windows look the same from outside, so long as the curtains are all lined in the same colour. Lining fabric is a specially woven sateen with a shiny side which is made up so it faces towards the window. It shrugs off dust and dirt, and is now available in a wide range of colours as well as in the natural and off-white most frequently used. Most linings are guaranteed pre-shrunk, but others are not, and if you buy one which is not pre-shrunk, wash it before using, otherwise it will pucker when the finished curtain is washed or dry-cleaned. Never be tempted to use a dress fabric or old curtain fabric for lining, it simply is not worth the effort. When making up lined curtains it is usual to make the linings slightly narrower by about $\frac{1}{2}$ inch (13 mm) inside the curtain edge, the lining hem about 1 inch (25 mm) above the curtain hem (independent of each other), and held by French tacks.

Make the curtains as described on the previous page up to stage 2, then cut the lining fabric slightly shorter than the curtain fabric, and seam the widths of the lining fabric together. Selvedges should also be snipped and seams pressed flat. Turn up hems of lining and machine stitch (unless you are going to hem them by hand), then, with the top edges of the curtain and linings together and seams aligned, lay the two layers of fabric out as flat as possible on the floor with the *wrong* side of the lining and the *wrong* side of the curtain facing each other. The lining now has to be 'locked' into position — you will need to make two rows of these on a 48 inch (1·20 m) wide curtain, three rows on a $1\frac{1}{2}$ width curtain, four on a double width and so on. For a single width curtain, turn back a third of the lining from one edge (*see above*) and work a row of long, loose blanket stitches down the fold, making sure no stitch shows on the right side of the curtain, finishing a few inches above the lower edge. Repeat the second row of 'locking stitches' one third from the other edge. If the curtain is wider, fold in half and 'lock' stitch down the centre, then fold right-hand side in half, 'lock' down centre and repeat for left-hand side. Turn up and stitch lining hems if sewing by hand. Make turnings about $1\frac{1}{2}$ inches (38 mm) wide along the outside edges of the curtains, press and tack. Turn in lining edge so the fold lies about $\frac{1}{2}-\frac{2}{3}$ inch (7–10 mm) inside the curtain edge, pin, tack and slip-stitch lining to the curtain, again making sure no stitches show on the right side.

Turn curtain and lining top over onto the wrong side, making sure that the lining and curtain fabric are as flat as possible (*right*), stitch on heading tape and continue making the curtains as previously described on pages 104/105. If the thickness seems too bulky (you will have five thicknesses including the tape) you can trim off the lining to reach only up to the

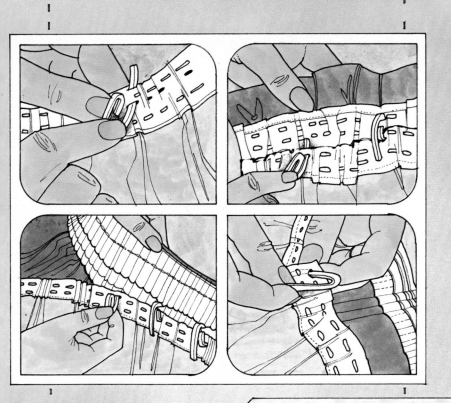

curtain fold.

Note. If you want to make *detachable* linings, so these can be removed for easy cleaning, there is a special detachable lining tape which can be used with all the different curtain styling tapes made by the same manufacturer. The curtains are made up as though unlined, the lining is made up with side and bottom hems and lining tape is sewn along the top. Curtain hooks pass through the small hole in the top edge of the lining tape and then through the pockets in the curtain tape, before being turned over into their final position (*above right*). Heavy curtains would still have to be 'locked' together and these stitches undone and resewn when necessary.

In a nursery, a detachable dark lining would be ideal for the summer months to shut out the daylight at bedtime!

What about Blinds?

There are two main types of window blind; venetian and roller. Venetians now come in a wide range of different colours, slat width and type, vertical as well as horizontal (see pages 86 and 87), and are generally used in conjunction with curtains. They help to insulate a room, so are ideal for large or north and east-facing rooms, and the horizontal type help make a narrow window look wider. Most venetian blinds are custom-made, you measure the window and give the shop all details, they forward the order to the manufacturer on your behalf. There are also some do-it-yourself venetian blind kits.

The roller blind too is now back in fashion, and is often an ideal treatment for awkward windows or glass doors, in a bathroom or kitchen for example. If you want privacy at night, but prefer sheer drapes, then a roller blind can be used *under* filmy curtains, or if you like an extra-dark bedroom, make a plain roller blind to complement patterned curtains, or vice versa. Blinds also come into their own in rooms where there are central heating radiators under the windows, but where elegant full-length curtains are required. Roller blinds can be made to come down to the sill or top of the radiators, in fabric to match, tone, or contrast with the floor-to-ceiling curtains. On nights when full benefit is needed from the radiators, the curtains are drawn to the radiator edge and the blinds pulled down.

Right: In a bedroom with a very small window a venetian blind has been used instead of curtains. The slats are in a shade of rich green and this colour is echoed in a band of paint which outlines the window.

Above: In this kitchen the roller blinds are used at the door as well as the window, and come from a range of easy-to-assemble blinds.

Far right: Blinds can be the answer to the radiator-under-a-window problem — at night pull the blinds down to the top of the radiator, but draw curtains to the radiator's edge or make 'false' curtains.

To Make a Roller Blind

First measure the window, using a yard stick if possible as this is rigid or alternatively a steel measure. First decide if the blind is to fit inside the window recess (or reveal) or go across it. Measure the width you want the finished blind to be and add on 3 in. (75 mm). Then measure the height adding on about 6 in. (150 mm). You will then need a roller blind kit consisting of: one top roller complete with winding gear; one *left* hand bracket with slot; one *right* hand bracket with round hole; one bottom slat; one end cap; one end spindle; one cord holder; one corn acorn; one length of cord; one lipped nail; screws and some tacks. If there is not one

available of the correct size to fit your window size, buy the next size up and cut it to fit. The maximum recommended drop for a 3 ft (90 cm) wide roller is 7 ft (210 cm), for a 4 ft (120 cm) roller 9 ft (275 cm), and for a 5 ft (150 cm) roller 10 ft (300 cm).

You will also need enough suitable fabric to make the blind. If possible, this should be wide enough without joining and slightly longer than the window height, plus the 6 ins (150 mm) — say an extra 12 ins (300 mm) — to allow for shrinkage. PVC coated fabrics are ideal, or glazed chintz or any firmly woven fabric such as linen, canvas, cotton sateen, etc. If you do have to join the fabric, buy double the amount and remember to allow for pattern matching if the fabric has a design. You will also need sewing thread to match fabric, or adhesive such as Copydex if using PVC, and trimming such as braid or fringe if required.

Start by fitting the roller. Screw the roller brackets to the window frame or walls (or ceiling if necessary); the bracket with the slot must go on the *left* and the one with the round hole on the *right*. If the brackets are face or wall fixed allow at least 1 inch (25 mm) from the ceiling to give clearance for the roller and fabric. The flanges should face inwards. Fix the left-hand bracket first, then slide the roller into the bracket and mark the position of the right-hand bracket. If the roller is too wide for the window you can cut it to the correct width at this stage, making sure you saw in a straight line. Sand down the rough edge, fit the metal end cap over the end and hammer in the nail so the lip is flush with the cap. Put the roller back in the brackets to check that it fits. Cut the fabric to fit the wood part of the roller, plus 3 inch (75 mm). If using ordinary fabric, turn in the hems and machine or hand stitch in the usual way. If you are

using PVC, cut the fabric only 2 inches (50 mm) wider than the roller and turn over a 1 inch (25 mm) fold down each side and stick down with the adhesive (only make one fold, don't turn in the raw edges as you would do with a fabric hem).

Cut the wooden slat to the correct width (same width as roller) and make a hem for this at the bottom of the fabric; machine stitch leaving the ends open, using a long stitch if the blind is PVC or again use adhesive or adhesive tape. Insert the slat in the hem and stitch up the ends. If required, the hem can now be trimmed with fringe or braid which is best stuck on with the adhesive.

Knot the cord at one end and pass the other through the acorn. Pass the cord through the cord holder and knot the other end. Screw the cord holder through the fabric and into the centre of the bottom slat with the screws provided. Tack the fabric to the roller so that the fabric is closest to the window. If you fit the fabric on the wrong way the blind will 'reverse wind' and the spring will fracture.

If the blind is ordinary fabric, turn back a 1 inch (25 mm) hem, right sides facing, at the top and press. Lay the blind on a flat surface with the right side facing you. Place the roller (spring on the *left* hand side) on the top edge of the blind and tack blind to roller with $\frac{1}{4}$ inch (6 mm) tacks following the line marked on the roller. Roll the blind up and place it in the brackets. Draw the blind down, to test the tension, by pulling the cord. When you gently pull the cord again the blind should roll up smartly but not too fiercely. If it does not do so, the tension needs tightening, so remove the blind and roller from the brackets, roll it up evenly by hand, replace and test again. Repeat if necessary. Never let the blind go up with a bang, ease it up with the cord.

Well Upholstered!

Upholstery is an ancient craft — the name originally meant 'upholder' or a person who hung tapestries on walls. The first 'upholstered' furniture was a simple wooden frame covered with animal skins, then leather and, later, homespun woollen and linen cloth. As furniture-making techniques advanced, expensive imported silks and velvets were used to cover springs and stuffing. The Victorians were the first to use almost every type of fabric for upholstery, to cover their voluptuously sprung and very over-stuffed furniture. They loved the rich texture of plush; the long-lasting qualities of leather and moquette; the rich gleam of satin; and used upholstery as an excuse to show off their skill at embroidery. Frames were sturdily made and there is many a Victorian chair waiting in the attic for a new lease of life!

Luckily, nowadays, with the development of foam and the introduction of upholstery fabrics in man-made fibres, the work of upholstering is much simpler, and it is possible to tackle certain jobs yourself. If you have never tried anything like this, start with a simple seat on a not-too-valuable chair; you may find one in a jumble sale or junk shop, to which you can give a complete 'face lift' with a few coats of bright paint and a gay cover (see illustration). Many modern armchairs have wooden arms and frames with loose cushions on a Pirelli Webbing base. These are also easy to upholster, as new webbing can be inserted, and the cushions (which are made of foam) can be easily re-covered using the existing cover as a pattern. Do not try to start on a complicated job such as a buttoned Chesterfield with sagging springs!

Choosing Fabrics

When making curtains it is important to choose a fabric which has been produced specifically for curtains, and the same is true with upholstery — as a general rule, dress fabrics are not suitable so don't be tempted by an odd remnant. Buy your upholstery fabric from a furnishing fabric department or through a shop specialising in curtains, carpets, interior decor and upholstery.

First of all look at the fabric for durability and strength. It should be firm to the touch, have a close weave and a surface from which dust may easily be brushed off. It should also be colour-fast, otherwise a small stain could spoil the appearance of the whole piece of furniture if the colour runs when an attempt is made to clean it, and strong sunlight will fade a non-colour-fast fabric very quickly. Try to get a small sample before you make up your mind, not only for colour-matching but for testing. Take it home and try washing or cleaning with a cleaning fluid, and if it stands the test then go

than Latex. It is best used on the resilient base, but the thinner the foam the firmer it must be to avoid discomfort in use. Again be guided by your supplier. Most Latex or Polyether foam can be stuck together with a special adhesive for extra thickness.

This chair is typical of the type used by our Victorian and Edwardian forefathers! Now upholstered in a rich brown velvet it looks really effective in a setting where matching fabric and wallcoverings have been used. There are still many chairs like this in attics, junk shops and jumble sales, waiting for you to bring them out, dust them down and re-cover them!

Far left: Two chairs as simple as ABC to renovate! The one at the top had a cane seat in holes — this was replaced with a piece of pierced hardboard, the frame was painted glossy black and signal red and a flat cushion, in pink, orange and red, dropped onto the hardboard. The lower chair was possibly once part of a Victorian breakfast room set; now this one remaining chair is given a new lease of life with a coat of paint and the drop-in seat reupholstered.

This beautifully upholstered windowseat in sage green velvet uses modern foam slabs for the cushion and back.

back and buy! Many modern fabrics contain some man-made fibres, or are specially treated before leaving the factory, so they are stain-resistant, often water-repellent and only need the occasional vacuuming or brushing; some even can be sponged down with a damp cloth. For your first attempt, choose a fabric which is not too expensive but not too cheap either, and make sure it is a fabric which you will find easy to work with. Usually velvets or any other cut-pile fabric, corded fabrics and leather or simulated leather need a practised hand!

Selecting Filling and Webbing

Often old springs can be re-used but they need lashing into place with webbing, and drop-in seats are often supported by webbing. There are two types; the rubber or Pirelli webbing which is resilient and is normally used in modern furniture, and the flax upholstery webbing which is firmer and is available in various qualities. Always tell your supplier exactly what you want it for and be guided by his advice.

Foam is an easy-to-handle filling, and comes in various types; Latex, which can be 'cavity sheet' (smooth skin with pattern of cavities underneath), 'pin-core' (pinhole cavities on the outside and generally used for square cushions) and 'plain sheet' (soft skin on both sides); Polyether or 'plastic' foam is available in a wide variety of thicknesses and is much cheaper

How do I Upholster a Chair?

The important thing to re-member is to start simple! The easiest chair to re-upholster is the dining room type, which just has an upholstered seat to cope with. These are usually the 'drop-in' (see previous page) or the 'stuff-over' type.

Drop-in Seat

This is the simplest seat of all to cover, but remember, the fabric for the new cover should not be any thicker than the original, otherwise the seat will not slot into place properly. In some instances the seat may have a solid base, but more often than not it will have a webbing base, covered with hessian. Strip off the old upholstery, carefully, as you can use this as a pattern for the new fabric, remove all the old tacks, clean and if necessary repair, and then re-web the frame following the step-by-step diagrams (**1–3**). Cover the bottom with hessian (**4**) then fit the upholstery foam (**5, 6**). Cut the new cover, using the old one as a pattern, but allowing a little more fabric, and use this to cover the seat, (**7**). Cut off any excess fabric and cover the seat bottom with a piece of linen or calico. Fold under raw edges, tack and slip seat into position.

Stuff-over Seat

This is the sprung type of chair which has webbing and cover-ing material attached directly to the rails of the chair. Remove the old upholstery as before, taking out tacks and repairing frame if necessary. Re-web the chair and cover with hessian as previously described. Take a sheet of stiff paper, cut out a pattern of the seat, allowing an extra $\frac{1}{2}$ inch (13 mm) all round, lay this on the smooth top of the foam which will be used for filling (this is easier than springs) and mark round with a ballpoint pen or with tailor's chalk until the pattern is transferred to the foam, cut the foam with a knife or the kitchen scissors dipped in water. Now lay the foam on the chair seat, cavity side down allowing an overlap of $\frac{1}{2}$ inch (13 mm) all round. Stick strips of calico to the outside edges on the top of the foam, making about 1 inch (25 mm) wide so that it can be pulled down and tacked to the seat rails using $\frac{3}{8}$ inch (10 mm) tacks. The cover should be at least $1\frac{1}{2}$ inch (38 mm) larger all round than the seat size to allow for turning in and tacking. Lay the cover over the seat and temporarily tack. This allows for correct positioning. Start at the centre front and work outwards, knocking in final tacks to within 2 inch (50 mm) of the front legs, and repeat the operation for the back and sides. At the corners cut out a V in the fabric, turn in the raw edge and tuck down the back legs, taking the folded end under the seat and tacking down. The front corners can be folded, cutting the surplus material away inside to give the fold a smooth finish. Gimp or braid can be used to trim the edge of the seat, being tacked with gimp pins or stuck with a latex adhesive.

To Button Upholstery

Many chairs and sofas have buttoned backs and this job is not nearly as difficult as it might look. You will need an uphol-stery needle (pointed both ends) and some strong twine or thread. Thread the needle, leaving 4-inch (100 mm) loose end; do not knot. Insert the needle into the upholstery, take the point as it emerges at the back, push through again to the front close to the insertion point, holding the thread tightly. Unthread the needle, pull the two threads tight, trim to an even length so they measure about 6 inch (150 mm) then thread the but-ton onto one of them. Tie a slip knot with the ends, pulling tight and push the button home into place, tying again. Cut thread ends about 1 inch (25 mm) from the button, wind round and tuck under button or push them into the fabric with the needle. *Above:* Two of the simplest chair seats to re-upholster; the drop-in and the stuff-over types.

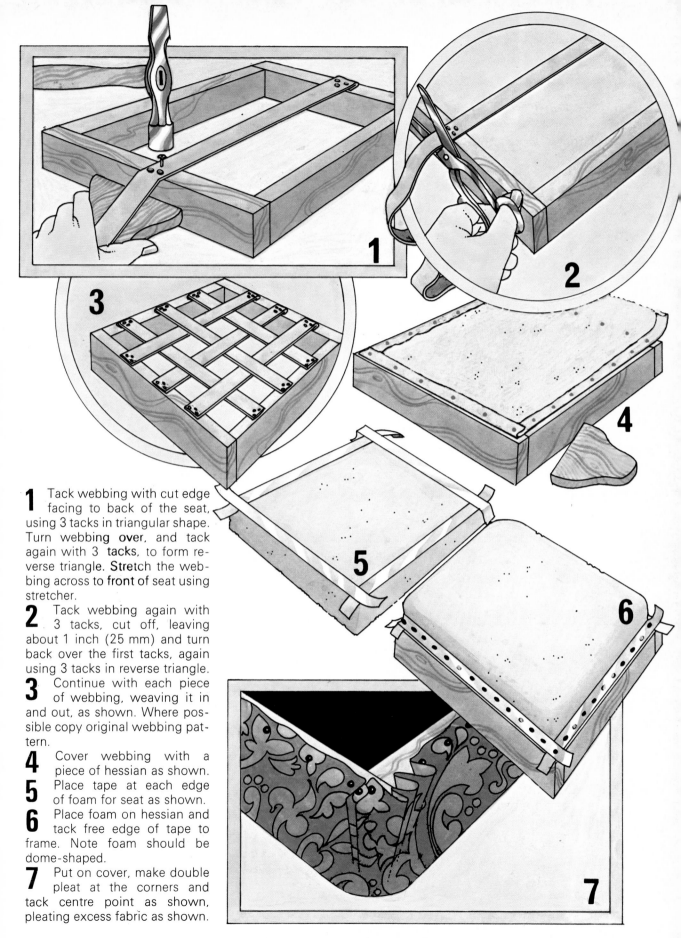

1 Tack webbing with cut edge facing to back of the seat, using 3 tacks in triangular shape. Turn webbing **over**, and tack again with 3 **tacks**, to form reverse triangle. **Stretch** the webbing across to **front** of seat using stretcher.

2 Tack webbing again with 3 tacks, cut off, leaving about 1 inch (25 mm) and turn back over the first tacks, again using 3 tacks in reverse triangle.

3 Continue with each piece of webbing, weaving it in and out, as shown. Where possible copy original webbing pattern.

4 Cover webbing with a piece of hessian as shown.

5 Place tape at each edge of foam for seat as shown.

6 Place foam on hessian and tack free edge of tape to frame. Note foam should be dome-shaped.

7 Put on cover, make double pleat at the corners and tack centre point as shown, pleating excess fabric as shown.

Cover-ups!

If upholstered furniture is in a good state of repair it may not need re-upholstering, but what if it does not fit into a new colour scheme? Up until fairly recently the only way of giving an old chair or settee a new look, without going to the bother or expense of re-upholstery, was to make a loose-cover. However nowadays it is possible to buy ready-made stretch-covers (see page 45) which fit well and are easy-care because the fabric is a jersey-knit type, generally made from a synthetic fibre. Unfortunately this type of fabric is not readily available for making one's own stretch-covers, so if your furniture is a problem shape you may well find you still have to make a loose-cover, although the stretch-cover manufacturers are increasing their ranges all the time and some will make special covers to order.

Making a Loose-cover

Again it is wise to start with a simple chair first, and then progress to the more difficult pieces. If the chair already has a loose-cover, then you can unpick this and use the pieces as a pattern, but remember to cut them slightly larger to allow for turnings. The fabric should be firmly-woven, crease- and shrink-resistant and colour-fast. If this is your first attempt at loose-covers, choose a plain material, or one with a very small pattern, since matching a large one can be quite difficult and wasteful of the fabric. Remember the

material must run from the top to the bottom on all sections of the cover.

If your chair does not already have a cover, then you will need to make a paper pattern first. With tailor's chalk, draw a line down the centre of the chair (you need only make a pattern for half the chair) (**1**). Pin the paper to the inside back with the edge on the chalk line. Keep it very smooth and even and allow 3 inches (75 mm) seams on top and sides and a good tuck-in of 6 inches (150 mm) round the

seat and curve of the arm. Mark curves with tailor's chalk or pencil. The seat pieces will have tuck-ins at sides and back and a turning in front. The lower front will require 3 inch (75 mm) turnings. Cut out the shape on the chair, and repeat for every other piece. Mark each piece to remind you of the direction of the pattern on your fabric to ensure it will be the correct way up on all pieces. Now arrange the pieces on the floor to conform to the width of the material chosen. The simplest way of planning the yardage is to clear a space on the floor and mark out on it a strip to represent the width of your material, using pins, string or tailor's chalk to indicate the strip of material. Be sure to keep the pieces to the pattern direction you have marked on them.

If possible, your material should be as wide as the widest part of the chair, plus turnings, to avoid joins. The seat, inside and outside back will be laid on a fold and all arm sections will be cut twice.

There is no need to make a pattern for a frill. If you need one calculate this as follows: measure round base of chair, treble this measurement to allow for pleating, divide total by width of material, taking the answer to the next largest whole number, then multiply by depth of frill + hems. This gives the material required in inches. This allows for box pleating, but if you require a frill which is gathered you should multiply instead by $1\frac{1}{2}$. Also allow material for piping; $\frac{3}{4}$ yard of 48 inch (685 mm of 1·20 m) wide material would give approximately 7 yards of $1\frac{1}{2}$ in (6·40 m of 38 mm) wide piping strips. Now add frill and piping quantities to the total required for your pattern pieces. (At your first attempt, do not rely on having sufficient waste strips for piping, but keep them in case a patch is ever needed).

Now cut all the pieces in the cover material, using your pattern as a guide. Mark all pieces as they are cut, on the wrong side of the material, B (Back), F (Front), RS (Right Side), etc, and T (Top) and B (Bottom), with tailor's chalk. Now pin all the pieces together, and fit on the chair, wrong side out (2). Make sure that the cover fits smoothly. To achieve this, snip curved seams, and adjust fullness by means of darts. Take the cover off the chair, trim off any surplus, and see that the cover is well pinned, so that you may easily turn it right side out. Fit it on the chair again as a final check before tacking.

Piping is optional, but does give a professional finish; most needlework books give full instructions. Now tack all seams, inserting piping where required (3). Stitch the seams, using the special piping foot on your sewing machine. When stitching heavy materials, such as repp, denim, etc, use a medium-coarse machine needle (17–18); 5 or 6 if sewing by hand, 12–8 stitches per inch.

Leave an opening on one of the back seams, at the base of the chair, and insert a zip fastener, press studs, or Velcro, so that the cover is easily fitted and removed.

It is a good idea to place a strip of cane, or a rolled newspaper, between the inner back and seat, pushed well down, and this will help to keep the cover smooth on the chair. Cut the frill pieces and join to give a continuous length. Hem the lower edge, and box pleat or gather. If pleated, press well before attaching to the cover. Tack piping to lower edge of cover, then stitch the top of the frill to this (4).

If you are not adding a frill to the cover, hem the lower edge. Attach tapes at each corner of the chair, tying them underneath. They will keep the cover tidy and it may still be removed easily when required.

Note: If you are covering two chairs of a suite, fit each one separately. Even though they are matching, there may be slight differences in shape due to wear.

Stretch-covers are now available in many different shapes, sizes, colours and designs, and some manufacturers will make to order for special chairs and settees (*above left*).

An attractive loose-cover can transform an old arm chair and give it a new lease of life (*left*).

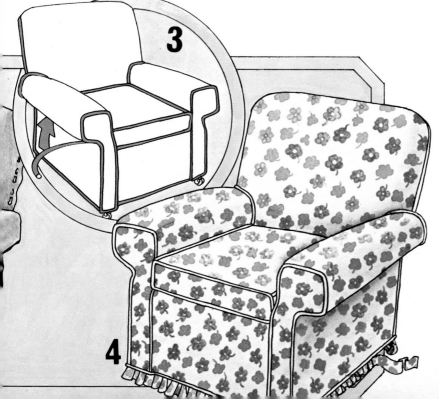

Can I Sew a Pretty Bedroom?

Once you have taken the plunge and started making your own curtains, soft furnishings are the next step! As can be seen from the pictures (opposite) curtain poles may be used for a variety of other purposes including a canopy over the bed, ideal for a small room where a four-poster would fit in with the decoration style, but might be too big and bulky. Simple throw-over bed-covers are not too difficult to make, and a room looks really effective with matching curtains and bedcover. Once you have tackled a simple design, you can then go on to more complicated covers.

For a pretty, feminine room, a kidney-shaped dressing table with a 'skirt' made from a layer of net or lace over an 'under-skirt' in taffeta, or another silky fabric, can again echo the curtain treatment, where frilled net cross-over drapes could be fitted *over* a plain roller blind in the same colour as the underskirt.

The important thing when making soft furnishings of this type is to choose a fabric which is easy to handle, does not fray quickly and is not too slippery. Again, just as with the curtains, use furnishing fabrics as opposed to dress fabrics, although it is not quite so important since they do not, as a general rule, have to stand up to the same amount of strong sunlight as curtains. From a practical point of view it is wise to choose fabrics which are washable, colourfast and shrink-resistant and, if you are adding decorative trimmings, see these have the same qualities. There is nothing worse than trimming a bedcover

with a bright braid or fringe only to find it runs the first time it is washed!

The simplest way to make this type of 'skirt' is to have a pair of short curtains, from the top of the table to just touch the floor; these divide in the centre to give access to the drawers. First remove the plate glass top from the table and use this to make a template to cut a top from the coloured fabric allowing about $\frac{1}{2}$ inch (13 mm) all round to turn in the raw edge. Turn in the raw edge, tack and hem. Place fabric on the top of the table and cover with the plate glass. Make your curtains from a layer of net over an underlayer of the coloured fabric, and sew Terylene tape to the top, then gather up and insert hooks. The fabric should be generously full so allow the measurement of the circumference of the table in *each* curtain. Fix flexible track to the table, just under the lip (Fig. 1) and insert hooks into gliders. It is a good idea to allow the cur-

fig 1

tains to hang before finally hemming.

Note. If your table does not have a plate glass top, you can get one cut or use a self-adhesive plastic to cover the top and lip, in a colour to match the under-skirt.

This basic throw-over bedcover (*below centre*) in a firm yellow linen-like furnishing fabric is trimmed with bands of mulberry coloured braid to match the gaily decorated whitewood furniture. Cushions in tones of mulberry, pink and red further enhance the scheme.

There are many different ways of making a bed canopy. A simple double width of net can be draped from a bracket or towel ring, and held each side of the bed with curtain bosses; or special coronets can be purchased and mounted on the wall or ceiling above the bed. In this picture (*left*), a curtain pole has been suspended from the ceiling and a pair of simple curtains form the drapes. A lavender bedcover with scalloped edge shows the pretty toning valance underneath, and the toning fabric is also used for tie-backs. A tiny pillow in the bedcover fabric, trimmed with lace, completes the scheme.

Far left: A simple idea for a bed without a headboard; a curtain pole is wall-mounted above the bed and a café-style curtain is made to match the bedcover and lampshade. The pillow is rolled in a small quilted cover in red and white spotted fabric which provides pattern contrast.

Above left: A kidney-shaped dressing table with ruched 'skirt' drawn up with curtain-heading tape looks pretty and feminine.

Finishing Touches

There is no doubt about it, the final finishing touches make a house into a home! If you have plenty of money and buy all your furniture new from a shop; employ an interior decorator to plan the schemes; have custom-made soft furnishings; even get your books 'by the yard', the chances are your home will lack individuality and personality and you will miss so much fun! Collecting pieces of furniture or *bric-a-brac*, restoring, painting, stripping, staining, converting them to suit your needs and tastes; these are what homemaking is all about and, when you look round the home, lovingly built up piece-by-piece through the years, you will have many happy memories and find you look on certain items as 'friends of the family'. You will discover, once you get bitten by the collecting bug, you cannot pass a charity or junk shop, jumble sale or white elephant stall without stopping to browse through everything offered for sale. The next step is the auction room (where there is still some chance of a lucky find) and the antique shop. Even though prices are going up all the time, you can still pick up some bargains so long as you know what to look for, or have the imagination to see what can be created from a discarded, sometimes broken-down piece of furniture!

What to Look For

First look at the structure and see whether it has been repaired and how well, decide whether it will need mending, and if so, ask yourself if you can tackle the job. A bargain is no longer a bargain if you have to pay a lot to have it professionally repaired, but don't dismiss upholstery as being beyond you. Today's materials have brought this craft within the scope of do-it-yourself (see Chapter 11). Large Victorian and Edwardian wardrobes can often be taken to bits and made into several new pieces of furniture, and so can old washstands, dressing tables, kitchen dressers, etc. so try to look at them with a fresh eye. Remember old wood often has a value of its own and, even if the furniture design is ugly, it

may be possible to reuse the wood. Look carefully at the finish; under coats of chipping paint there may be a gleam of really good mahogany, oak or pine, well worth stripping and waxing, while other 'treacly' finishes attempt to hide a poor piece of wood. Avoid furniture with badly chipped veneer (a thin sliver of wood used to cover the stronger base wood) as this is hideously difficult to repair and the chips are still noticeable even if you cover them with countless coats of paint.

Try to learn as much about furniture and wood as you can by reading books, visiting stately homes and museums, looking round quality antique shops; the more you know the more likely you are to find a bargain. Always examine wood for traces of

woodworm, and this includes the frame of any upholstered furniture. It is not really a worm, but a beetle which lays eggs in the wood, then the grubs hatch and gnaw their way through and finally fly away to lay their eggs in another piece of wood. If you bring one untreated piece into your home, sooner or later every piece of woodwork, including doors, skirtings and floors can become infected. In mild cases, the wood will have small round holes and possibly a little powdery wood dust will be noticeable under the piece of furniture. In advanced cases the wood is so peppered with holes it looks rather like honeycomb and eventually crumbles away. You can treat the first type yourself with one of the proprietary solutions on the market, but you *must* deal with it before you bring the furniture into the house; outside on concrete is best, or in the garage. The severe case cannot be treated successfully, so don't buy the item unless you can renew the affected part (burn this at once), again before bringing the piece of furniture indoors.

There are other items well worth hunting for, quite apart from wood or upholstered furniture; pieces of china and pottery, glass, copper and brass (often so tarnished it is not recognizable), chrome, marble, metal, old mirrors and pictures, cooking implements, even discarded furniture, can all be given a new lease of life with a bit of work and care,

so don't pass them over.

A word of warning! Don't tamper with a genuine antique, and this includes some old painted and lacquered pieces, as you could completely ruin them. If in doubt ask advice of an expert, either at your local shop, or various museums will help if you can send a photograph of the piece to them. Never paint really good wood as this can spoil it, and don't paint metal unless you are sure it is *not* copper, bronze, brass or silver, again, if in doubt, seek advice.

These pictures show just what can be done with junk shop finds! A cast-iron Victorian 'pub' table (*far left*) was rubbed down and repainted gloss white. The chair was mended, the old cane seat removed and replaced by pierced hardboard, the frame painted and the slim cushion added. The china fruit bowl was another bargain buy at a jumble sale, and to complete the scheme, lampshade and wastepaper basket were made from scraps of left-over wallcovering.

Above: In this modern bathroom the dressing table is a converted sewing-machine stand, painted white, and topped with a marble slab taken from a Victorian washstand. Old treadle-type sewing machines are well worth looking out for even though the actual sewing machine may be useless.

Left: An Edwardian washstand with marble top was found in an old barn; the wood was in need of some repair, but the marble top and tiled back rail were in good condition. The wood was stained red, the marble and tiles cleaned and refurbished, and now it makes a handy desk in the corner of a family room.

Cleaning, Stripping, Staining and Painting

Many old pieces of furniture do not need drastic treatment to bring them back to their former glory, so do not immediately rush at your new find with scraper and blowlamp! First of all give it a good clean, but this does not mean swamping it with water and detergent. First try cleaning with a soft cloth which has been wrung out after soaking in warm water and mild detergent; the cloth should only be damp, not wet. Another good cleaning method for furniture with a build-up of polish is to mix 1 part turpentine or turpentine substitute, 1 part water and 1 part vinegar in a bottle; shake well and then sprinkle some of the mixture lightly on to a soft cloth (again do not make it too wet) and rub the furniture all over with this. Once the furniture is clean, you can see whether you need to treat scratches, dents, burns, water marks, mend damaged areas of veneer, or touch up french polish or varnish. Many helpful books are available which give hints on coping with these problems.

Stripping

If, having cleaned the piece, you decide it needs stripping, the best thing to do is use a proprietary chemical stripper suitable for the particular finish you want to remove, your local do-it-yourself shop should be able to advise you. Follow the instructions which come with the stripper and remember, because it is a chemical, it will be highly caustic. Try to work outside, in a garage, or well ventilated room; protect the surrounding area from splashing, but protect yourself by wearing glasses, rubber gloves and protective clothing. Wash any spots of chemical off immediately with cold water. Work away from pets and children and make sure they cannot touch or drink the stripper, or knock it over if you leave it for a moment to answer the door or telephone. Work on a small area at a time, following the instructions, and you should find the stripper will lift and soften the film on the furniture, but sometimes you may have to use a scraper. If the piece is carved you can use an old toothbrush to work the solution round the crevices, and a knitting needle is useful for getting into odd corners. Clean down the stripped furniture, preferably with methylated spirit or turpentine substitute (if stripping instructions allow it) rather than water. Fill any holes, carry out any repairs and you are then ready to wax, oil, polish, bleach, lime, fume, stain, seal, to taste.

Note. Always do a test piece first (somewhere where it will not be too obvious), before treating wood in any way, to make sure you are not going to do more harm than good.

Staining

Stained furniture can look most effective (see illustration on previous page) as the lovely grain of the natural wood shows through the rich colour. Jewel shades are available, but wood can also be stained in various tones to match other wood such as light or dark oak, mahogany etc. Unless the wood is untreated whitewood, or you have stripped and bleached it, the original colour of the wood is likely to affect the finished colour, so do a small test piece first where it will not show if you decide not to use stain. Stains are improving all the time and there is a choice of several different types on the market. All stains should be applied to smooth, clean, dry wood, using a brush, soft cloth or sponge. Apply evenly, working with the grain, allow to dry, apply a second or even third coat if

required, and then finish with a wood sealer to heighten the colour and protect the wood. Some stains are applied direct from the bottle or tin, others have to be mixed with water, and for brighter colours and deeper penetration some can be mixed with half water and half methylated spirits, but be guided by the maker's instructions.

Painting

If, after cleaning, you decide the wood of your piece of furniture is not good enough to leave as it is, and the grain is not interesting enough for you to want it to show through a stain, painting is the best possible way of creating an attractive finish and one which will blend speci-

fically with your decorations. Much has been written about the techniques of painting, but one point is worth saying again, proper preparation is essential! If you have a poorly prepared surface the finished job will look cheap and nasty, however nice the piece of furniture and whatever paint you use. All furniture should be thoroughly sanded down with glass-paper on a sanding block or sanded with a power tool, until the surface is smooth. Any holes should be filled, the filler rubbed down smoothly, the whole piece should then be dusted down, wiped over with a fairly damp cloth to remove all fine particles and left to dry. Any knots should be treated with knotting

solution, and then the whole piece primed. Leave it to dry, rub down and remove all dust, then apply the first undercoat, rub it down when dry, again remove all dust, apply a second undercoat if necessary and so on until you have a really good finish. It is most important to keep the area round the furniture dust-free while you are working on it and while it is drying for a sudden breeze could completely spoil your handiwork!

Illustrations

Furniture does not have to be old, as these modern decorated whitewood pieces show, some are painted and others are stained (*See left*).

Top left: Same chest, two colourways! The trick here is to do the undercoat over the whole piece, suitable for the lighter colour, then sketch the design with pencil or chalk. Paint the top coat in the lighter colour first and the darker colour will cover up any stray brush marks.

Top right: Old circular room tables which have a tip-up top can still be found fairly cheaply. Some are in good wood, like mahogany, and should not be painted; others in a more homely finish can be painted very successfully, using the method described on this page.

Left: Old garden furniture can be given a new lease of life with a coat of paint.

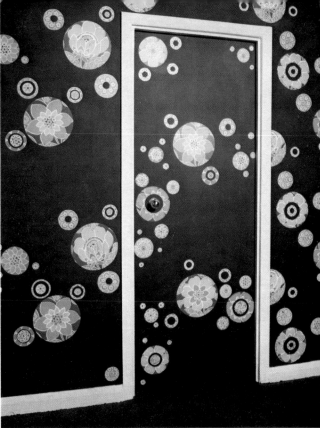

Ideas Unlimited!

There are lots of other ways of creating interesting finishing touches without necessarily doing up old furniture or resorting to the paintbrush! You may find you have a dull room scheme which can be brightened up considerably by the clever use of 'accent' colours, introduced in accessories (for more details see pages 30, 31) and you can work wonders with painted patterns on walls (pages 62, 63) and various other *trompe l'oeil* tricks, but the same effects can be used to renovate furniture, disused biscuit tins, mirrors, pictures, even an old electric fire

can become an integral part of the colour scheme!

If you are not at all handy with a paintbrush, then try cutting and sticking! There are lots of good self-adhesive plastics available, and some now come in mix-and-match ranges so it is possible to create the most amazing effect with very little trouble and effort as can be seen from some of our pictures. Wallpaper can be used in more ways than one too; if it has a distinct pattern, then this can be cut out and used as a motif to decorate furniture, doors, boxes and so on, and is one way of making a child's room particularly gay. Long strips of wallpaper or self-adhesive plastics make very good friezes too, which can be used as bands of colour (like the painted stripes on the previous page) round doors, and across walls, as well as in the more usual place between wall and ceiling, or to accent or simulate a picture rail. I hope the ideas on these two pages will give you the inspiration to have a go at making a few interesting finish-

ing touches for your home.

Brighten up the bedroom! Conventional bedheads can be expensive, here are two ideas (*above*) which should be fairly cheap. The first bedhead is made from a 1930's mirror, taken off a dressing table which was part of a conventional bedroom suite. The dressing table now stands in the window with a free-standing mirror on top, which cuts daylight less and is much more flexible.

When a bed is pushed up to an old chimney breast once the fireplace has been removed, it is possible to do all sorts of exciting things with cushions to make a bedhead. A curtain pole, with cushions suspended from it for example, is one tried and tested way, but here two cushions in a cloud shape and design have been fixed to the wall at head height.

When is a door not a door? In a room with many doors (*above*), this is a good way of disguising them so they merge into the background. The walls have been papered with a fairly bold

design, and the doors are painted to match the background colour of the paper. Some of the motifs have been cut out from left-over pieces of paper and stuck on the door to echo the pattern on the paper on the surrounding wall area. Much more practical than trying to stick paper on to doors!

Finishing touches with cut-and-stick! Self-adhesive plastic can be used as decorative borders to brighten up a kitchen. The best way to apply this type of plastic to the wall is to use the detergent technique. 1. Using a normal solution of washing-up liquid and water, wet the wall. 2. Carefully strip off 3 ft (1 m) of backing paper from a length of self-adhesive plastic cut to size. 3. Stick *lightly* in position as accurately as possible. Overlap with previous piece by about $\frac{1}{4}$" (6 mm). Do not butt join. 4. Firmly holding this section with one hand, strip off the rest of backing paper and press the self-adhesive plastic in place, repositioning and trimming as necessary. Smooth out or prick bubbles.

More ways with self-stick; (*right*): the most battered object can be given a new lease of life if it is cleaned and imaginatively covered with self-stick plastic.
P.S. Even an old electric fire gets the treatment, with paint. The fire must be in good working order and you must take great care not to splash or damage the elements in any way, also do not paint too near the element area as the paint could discolour or even burn. Clean the fire thoroughly, allow to dry, prime with metal primer if necessary, then paint with top-quality gloss paint following instructions on pages 120 and 121. Remember to switch off and unplug before doing any of this!

Pretty as a Picture!

Most people have a few pictures or prints which they want to display on their walls, but all too often these are badly hung! If you have a really good picture, then this could well be the focal point of a room by placing it against a richly-

This picture shows just how effective a few simple items can look, grouped together on a side table — flower decoration blends perfectly with the design on the lamp base.

If you want to **show off** several prints, pictures, photographs etc. try massing them on one wall in a really eye-catching arrangement.

coloured or interestingly textured wall and making sure it is properly lit (spotlights are best, see page 92 and 93). On the other hand, nothing looks worse than a room with one picture on each wall, placed far too high to be appreciated, and one of the greatest decorating sins is to place a picture or mirror centrally over the fireplace!

Good grouping of pictures and treasures plays a most important part in the final finishing touches to a room scheme, and you may well find you have to group and regroup them before the effect is just right. Pictures, prints, wall hangings, etc. all look much better massed together on one wall, possibly round a clock or mirror. It is better to have a completely uncluttered and under-accessorised room than one where the 'bits and pieces' are wrong, but this does not mean a stark, modern decoration scheme has to have just one geometric picture on the wall. You can really have great fun collecting an odd assortment of items, refurbishing them where necessary and using them to add interest to the scheme. Plants too, can be used

as accessories to create a softening effect.

Make your own Wallhangings!

There is nothing quite so rewarding as creating your own pictures, but if you are not very good at drawing and painting the results can be disappointing. However there are now many craft ideas which can be translated into pictures and wallhangings — collage; embroidery; macramé; paper sculpture; corn dollies; block printing; natural dyeing; tie-and-dye; batik, for example. Books on craft and magazine articles give helpful instructions for most of these, but probably two of the most fascinating, and easiest to do, are tie-and-dye and batik using Cold Dyes. (For dyeing details see pages 54 and 55).

The red and orange picture was made as follows. A piece of cotton fabric measuring 18" (45 cm) by 18" (45 cm) was tied ready for dying. The centre point of the square was picked up to form a peak, the fabric furled like an umbrella and bound downwards from the point for $1\frac{1}{2}$" (4 cm) then at $1\frac{1}{2}$" intervals to a depth of 7" (18 cm). Each corner was picked up and a separate binding was put on these, about 2" (5 cm) deep. The whole was dyed in Nasturtium Cold Dye, then rinsed and dried. Bindings were widened and the whole dyed in Camillia Cold Dye. This was then rinsed and dried, the bindings untied and the fabric ironed on the wrong side. The picture was then framed in a simple natural wood frame with white mount.

The batik wallhanging *above left* was also made using Cold Dyes, wax and a piece of linen. To make one yourself:

1 Wash and iron the fabric to remove any dressing as this will prevent the dye penetrating thoroughly. Use a soft pencil, draw your design on to the fabric, or trace an outline from a magazine placed under the fabric.

2 Stretch the fabric over a batik frame or old picture frame and secure with drawing pins. Melt some candle wax in an old saucepan and apply to the fabric with a paintbrush to the areas you do *not* wish to dye. As the wax hardens the fabric takes on a transparent appearance. Remove fabric from frame.

Starting with the lightest colour, mix the Cold Dye in accordance with the instructions. Thoroughly wet the fabric in cold water and immerse it in the dye solution for up to one hour, depending on the depth of colour required, stirring constantly for the first 10 minutes and then occasionally to ensure even penetration of the dye. Remove fabric from the dye, rinse in cold water until it runs clear and drip-dry away from heat.

3 When dry re-pin fabric to frame and apply more hot wax where you wish to retain the first dye and keep out the next dye colour. Mix second Cold Dye colour, wet fabric in cold water and dye as before. If more than two colours are required, continue until pattern is complete.

4 When dyeing is complete, rinse in cold water and drip-dry. Iron off the wax between wads of absorbent paper then wash in a bowl of hot detergent. Rinse, dry, iron and hang.

Note. Never pour waxy water down the sink.

Acknowledgements

I should like to thank the following firms for their help in preparing this book — without their beautiful pictures to prove the points made in the text, this book would not have been so colourful or visually stimulating.
I would also like to thank Lizi Freeman who took on the gruelling task of photographic research for me.

The Sure and Simple Series consists of 5 unique guides to Home Improvements, Gardening, Cooking and Crafts.

The amateur thinking of tackling an unfamiliar job in the house or garden will find these books invaluable.
Each one has been written by an expert who knows how to avoid the common pitfalls and is able to give explanations in clear, non-technical language. Each page has been carefully designed, and every step is illustrated with diagrams and easy to follow text.
The homemaker with neither much time nor much money will also find that this series is full of helpful hints which enable him to achieve professional results quickly, easily and cheaply.

SURE AND SIMPLE HOME MAKING by Jill Blake
Includes hints on planning, flooring, lighting, curtains and blinds, upholstery, coping with colour, schemes that work and finishing touches which give a home that extra special 'something'.

SURE AND SIMPLE COOKING by Alison Burt
A complete basic cookbook including a varied collection of interesting recipes for puddings and cakes, sauces, pasta and rice, meat and poultry, soups, fish dishes and herbs and spices.

SURE AND SIMPLE DO-IT-YOURSELF by Harry Butler
All aspects of maintaining and improving your home are covered including woodworking, decorating, plumbing, electricity, insulating, bricklaying, concreting and masonry, repairs and maintenance.

SURE AND SIMPLE GARDENING by Geoffrey Smith
A comprehensive gardening book covering vegetable gardening, lawn care, roses, pests and diseases, propagation, rock and water gardens, trees and shrubs and indoor plants.

HOMECRAFTS by Eve Harlow
An absorbing introduction to ten popular crafts: decoupage, corn dollies, stained glass, patchwork and quilting, pressed and dried flowers, block printing, batik, natural dyeing, Ikebana and pottery.